THE
YIDDISH
FOLKSONG
PROJECT
ANTHOLOGY

The arrangements of Robert De Cormier

Volume I
18 Songs

THE YIDDISH FOLKSONG PROJECT ANTHOLOGY

The arrangements of Robert De Cormier

Volume I
18 Songs

With downloadable MP3s

Restored and in new versions for voice and piano by John Yaffé

Edited and Compiled by
John Yaffé

Author's corrections in red. *J.Y.*

ipsilon
music press

First published in the United Kingdom in 2020
by Ipsilon Music Press

For Europe:
The Postbox
53 Upper Marshall Street
Birmingham B1 1LA (UK)

For the Americas:
604 Riverside Drive, Suite 3-C
New York, NY 10031 (U.S.A.)

www.ipsilonmusic.com

Library of Congress Cataloging-in-Publication Data

Yaffé, John, 1952–
The Yiddish Folksong Project: The arrangements of
Robert De Cormier, Volume I / John Yaffé. — 1st UK ed.

British Library Cataloguing-in-Publication Data

A catalogue record for this book is available from the
British Library

ISBN 978-1-5272-4695-9
LCCN 2019914101
1. Jewish music. 2. Yiddish folk song—Arrangements.
3. Yiddish singing diction—Pronunciation. 4. Robert De
Cormier

Music engraving by Ipsilon Music Services, New York
and Birmingham (UK)

Design by Blind Mice Design, Coventry (UK)

Printed in the United Kingdom by Page Bros Print,
Norwich

*Publication of this book was made possible in large part
through the generosity of The Endeavor Foundation*

Cover image:
Marc Chagall, 'Libération', detail from the triptych
'Résistance, Résurrection, Libération'
(Musée national Marc Chagall, Nice, France)

Dedicated to the memory of Robert De Cormier
(1922-2017)

The Downloadable MP3s

All songs in this volume are available as either (one-time) downloadable MP3 files or on a physical CD. These tracks are available to you at no charge if you have purchased a copy of this volume. If you have not purchased this volume, you can order the tracks from the publisher or from an online music store.

The download (or CD) contains two sets of audio tracks:

- versions with voice and accompaniment
- versions with only the accompaniment

The former is intended for the listener's pleasure and/or as a study aid. From them, users of this volume will have an opportunity to clearly hear the Yiddish text sung, familiarize themselves with the music, and get a general sense of the style of each song. The latter set of tracks has the purpose of affording the singer an opportunity (a) to practice the songs with accompaniment before starting rehearsals with their pianist and/or (b) to use the files as 'backing tracks', should they need/wish to perform them without piano.

NOTE: Although the recordings are of the version for voice, piano, and violin, the musical content is the same as that found in the current voice-and-piano version.

OPTION A

1. Go to the following Web address: www.ipsilonmusic.com/yfsp

2. Follow the instructions found there.

OPTION B

To get the audio files in CD form, do the following:

1. E-mail a copy of your proof of purchase to info@ipsilonmusic.com (be sure to include your shipping address).

2. We will ship the CD to the address given.

Other Versions Available

In addition to the arrangement for voice and piano in this anthology, the songs are also available from the publisher in the following versions:

- **Voice and instrumental ensemble**
  Flute, oboe, clarinet, percussion, harp, accordion, and string quartet
  (Robert De Cormier's original scoring)

- **Voice, violin, and piano**
  (reduction by John Yaffé)

Transpositions

Transpositions (into any key) of any of the songs in this anthology can be ordered from the publisher (e-mail: info@ipsilonmusic.com)

The songs in this volume were first performed live by **Juliana Janes-Yaffé**, soprano, with instrumental ensemble conducted by **John Yaffé**, at the Plymouth Church of the Pilgrims, New York City, on March 13, 2005.

The MP3 recordings associated with this volume were made in the spring and summer of 2016 at **Henry Wood Hall**, London, with **Juliana Janes-Yaffé**, soprano, **John Yaffé**, pianist, and **Adam Summerhayes**, violinist. Recording, editing, and mixing engineer: **Patrick Allen**

Acknowledgments

This publication owes a debt of gratitude to the following for helping to make its release possible:

- The late Robert De Cormier, whose superb arrangements inspired and are the focus of this project;

- the late singers Marthe Schlamme and Netanya Davrath, whose recordings of Yiddish folksongs first brought our attention to the De Cormier arrangements;

- soprano and voice pedagogue Juliana Janes-Yaffé, for her invaluable advice on the IPA song transliterations and pronunciation guides in the Anthology, for her musical expertise and artistry in the accompanying recording of the songs, and for her overall good counsel throughout the project;

- acclaimed author, humourist, and 'Yiddishist' Michael Wex, for scrutinizing the English translations of the songs in this anthology, and for adding an additional layer of insight into the meaning of particular words, expressions, phrases, and cultural traditions;

- Yiddish folksong experts Zalmen Mlotek, Jascha Nemtsov, and Maddy Simon for sharing their valuable time and knowledge;

- recording editing, and mixing engineer Patrick Allen, whose own musical skill, level-headedness, technical mastery, and dedication to this project made the recording process a pleasure;

- Julie Kidd, President of The Endeavor Foundation, for taking the project to heart, realizing its significance, and lending both moral and financial support to it;

- Dr. Lori McCann, Associate Professor of Voice at the John J. Cali School of Music, Coordinator of Voice Program, Montclair State University (New Jersey), for applying her keen pedagogical eye to the content and execution of this volume; and

- all the universities, organizations, conference organizers, concert presenters, synagogues, churches, cathedrals, and schools that encouraged the project by affirming their belief that this repertoire should be introduced to as many people as possible.

Contents

'*Jewish song has always accompanied the history of the Jewish people. The expression of the soul of the Jewish people is in their song; more correctly: it IS their song.*'

— **Elie Wiesel**, Nobel Prize-winning author

Foreword

We sing folksongs to our children. We are touched when a singer offers a folksong at the end of an evening of sophisticated art song. Few forms of vocal music span such a wide range of experience.

Yet the world of folksong can easily daunt us. Can we truly enter the directness, the 'authenticity', the naïveté even, of this literature? Not least when it derives, as here, from one of the most specifically defined cultures of our world?

This superb collection opens up the world of Yiddish folksong to all, explaining context and pronunciation, providing effective piano accompaniments that can be realized by professional and amateur alike, and giving us a glimpse of the breadth of reference in this music. Though most of these songs are strophic, the repetitions are varied subtly, and the use of a variety of keys (yes, even major keys!) makes it easy to put together a varied programme for any context.

An important part of this project is the inclusion of recordings of performances featuring voice, violin, and piano. Soprano Juliana Janes-Yaffé sings these songs with an admirable fusion of purity and passion. These performances celebrate the dance origins of much of the music, yet also the deep seriousness of this heritage. We are of course moved by the defiant 'Zog nit keynmol', created in the midst of the Holocaust. But we are also touched by songs like the first one in the book, 'A dudele', with the singer's fervent, respectful, yet intimate personal dialogue with God ('du'). The directness and sincerity of Ms. Janes-Yaffé's performance, as with her collaborators John Yaffé (pianist) and Adam Summerhayes (violinist), will inspire all who use this volume as a basis for their own discoveries. It has opened a new world to me, and will assuredly do the same for you.

David Syrus
Head of Music (1993-2017)
Royal Opera House, Covent Garden

Preface

This anthology constitutes Volume I of the Yiddish folksong arrangements of eminent American arranger-conductor-composer Robert De Cormier (1922–2017). It introduces — for the first time in published form — eighteen of the forty-four arrangements forged by De Cormier between 1957 and 1963 for three Vanguard Records LP recordings by two different singers: Marthe Schlamme (1957 and 1959) and Netanya Davrath (1963). The original arrangements were crafted for voice with an accompaniment ranging from one to ten instruments, depending on the song.

In the early research and restoration phase of this project, it was discovered that the manuscript materials used by De Cormier and the instrumentalists for the original Vanguard recordings had been taken home by De Cormier immediately after the sessions, where they languished in a storage cupboard for more than forty years, and that those arrangements *had never been performed live*. As a result of an agreement between De Cormier and this author, further restoration and research on the arrangements took place and has blossomed into the foundation-funded *Yiddish Folksong Project*, the mission of which includes:

- the restoration of all forty-four De Cormier arrangements;

- their performance worldwide;

- a series of lectures and lecture-recitals placing Yiddish folk song in its cultural and historical context;

- the assurance (through publication) that the songs/arrangements are available to other trained singers worldwide, in performable versions, in perpetuity; and

- a wider dissemination of Yiddish folk song in general.

The first step in the restoration of the arrangements was to collate all the disparate manuscript materials — scores and parts — making sure that the materials for each song were present. Then, the original pencil/pen manuscript notation had to be computerized in a state-of-the-art music notation programme, meticulously edited and corrected, song-by-song; the vocal parts and their corresponding Yiddish texts (mostly missing from the original scores) had to be transcribed from the LPs or researched externally; the raw musical content had to undergo an aural comparison with the original recordings, to assure that the notation represented the arranger's and performer's intentions; and the sum total of text and music transformed into new engravings suitable for rehearsal (including a piano reduction), performance, and publication.

Thus, the book you are holding is the first of its kind. As of this writing, we know of no other anthology of Yiddish folksong arrangements with this volume's distinctive features:

- a large collection of finely-crafted concert arrangements of Yiddish folk songs by a single, recognized composer-arranger;

- intended to be sung in the original Yiddish by trained singers;

- available in the following versions: (a) piano and voice (the version found in this volume); (b) piano, violin, and voice; and (c) instrumental ensemble and voice (Robert De Cormier's original scoring);

- with a comprehensive set of pedagogical components, such as a Yiddish pronunciation guide, a comparison of Yiddish and German, a brief history of the Yiddish language, and a three-pronged translation of each song text: (a) an IPA (International Phonetic Alphabet) transliteration, (b) a word-for-word translation, and (c) an 'idiomatic' translation; and

- downloadable MP3 recordings of all songs in this volume, both in *sung* versions and in *accompaniment-only* versions (as aids to learning the songs). Also available in CD form.

With the release of this anthology, professional singers, singers-in-training, répétiteurs (coaches), and singing teachers will now have access to a wonderful new body of vocal literature from a pedagogically conceived publication. It is our sincere hope that singers around the world will heartily embrace this repertoire, enchant their audiences with it, and become participants in the broader dissemination of this rich cultural and musical heritage to a global community.

John Yaffé
January 2020
Birmingham, England

Folksong Arrangement and Dissemination, 'The Yiddish Folksong Project', and the Questions of Style and Authenticity

Folksong Arrangement and Dissemination

For the past 100 years, many dedicated researchers and archivists have collected and transcribed Yiddish folk song melodies and texts. Many of these have been given cursory arrangements (with accompaniment) in some Yiddish song anthologies and by composers of the 'New Jewish School' (also known as the 'St. Petersburg School') of the early twentieth century. Even some well-known composers have tried their hand at musicalizing Yiddish. Dmitri Shostakovich used Yiddish texts but created original melodies on them; Darius Milhaud composed all his *Poemes Juifs* to French translations of Yiddish; and Maurice Ravel's two settings altered the original modal melodies. Others such as Viktor Ullmann, and Stefan Wolpe tried their hand at setting (intact) Yiddish folksong melodies, but their combined output amounts to less than a dozen songs, and their settings can hardly be said to be illuminating.

Unfortunately, the exposure of Yiddish folksong to a wider public has been limited owing to the relative lack of performance of such songs in regular, mainstream international recital performance. In contrast to this, folk songs of certain other cultures have gained worldwide popularity by way of the masterful concert arrangements some well-known composers have made of the songs of their homelands. Just to name a few:

- Between 1858 and 1894, Johannes Brahms did more than 100 arrangements of German folk songs;

- between 1872 and 1886, Antonin Dvorak did more than forty-five arrangements of Czech folk songs;

- between 1904 and 1949, Ralph Vaughan Williams collected and arranged hundreds of folk songs of England, Scotland, Wales, Ireland, as well as France, Germany, and Italy;

- between 1906 and 1946 Béla Bartók did nearly 100 arrangements of Hungarian, Rumanian, Slovak, and Ukranian folk songs;

- between 1923 and 1930, Joseph Canteloube did thirty arrangements of French folk songs of the Auvergne region;

- between 1950 and 1952 Aaron Copland did ten arrangements of American folk songs; and

- between 1941 and 1976, Benjamin Britten did more than fifty arrangements of folk songs of the British Isles.

Folksong Arrangement
and Dissemination, 'The
Yiddish Folksong Project',
and the Questions of
Style and Authenticity
(Continued)

Such composers embraced the folk songs of their homelands and applied their compositional ingenuity to them in the form of arrangements suitable for concert performance. However, until recently, the repertoire has lacked a significant body of finely crafted arrangements of Yiddish folk songs — arranged by a single composer — that would attract trained singers to this important literature.

Most anthologies of Yiddish song are rendered in 'lead sheet' form. These renderings (melody and text only) are useful for archival and research purposes, but any use of them for performance purposes requires the hand of a musician able to flesh them out into viable accompaniments for the desired musicians. As such, the songs are subject to the unpredictability of the one whose hand is responsible for the arranging. The existing published examples of Yiddish folk songs with piano accompaniment are generally in cursory arrangements, and those volumes include no supplementary teaching aids to help the professional singer, singer-in-training, or singing teacher, with this less-familiar language.

It is the belief of this author that, for all the above reasons, the dissemination of this slice of cultural heritage has been extremely limited. It has, unfortunately, remained caught within the small circles of Jewish families, congregations, social events, archives, klezmer camps, and conferences on Yiddish music. These songs have had relatively little exposure to the world outside these small circles, *because they have not been disseminated through the channels by which all other significant song repertoire gets its global exposure: the thousands of song recitals performed by trained student and professional singers each year around the world.* Thus, it is significant to mention here that without those concert arrangements of folk songs by the composers mentioned above, there would be a significant body of folksong literature sequestered within the songs' respective cultural circles, in scholarly archives, and possibly amongst some folk music enthusiasts, completely unknown to a large portion of the global public — or at least the global concert-going public.

'The Yiddish Folksong Project'

In 1999, at the conclusion of a vocal competition in New York City, the three Vanguard LPs mentioned in the 'Preface' to this volume were brought to the attention of the competition award recipient, soprano Juliana Janes-Yaffé. Her recognition of the significance of the songs on those recordings, in arrangements crafted by Robert De Cormier, was immediate. Fortuitously, it was at that point in time that she had been considering what the profile of her next solo recital programme might be, and she decided that *this* should be it: a programme made up entirely of De Cormier's marvelous Yiddish folksong arrangements; a programme that would, for the first time ever, introduce the concert-going public to this musically excellent, thematically varied, culturally significant, passionate, poignant, poetic, philosophical, playful, sometimes-disturbing-but-always-heartfelt slice of the vocal repertoire.

It is significant to mention here that when referring to Robert De Cormier — conductor, arranger, and composer — we are referring to one of the most highly regarded American musicians of the second half of the twentieth century. His name was synonymous with choral music across the six-decade span of his career. Moreover, he was a major player in the politically charged 'folk music revival' of the 1950s and 60s, and his contribution to the editing, arranging, performing, and publishing of folksong literature *in general* is immeasurable.

The magic of De Cormier's arrangements lies in the inventiveness and integrity of their composition while still maintaining the 'accessibility' of folk music. De Cormier demonstrates a sensitivity to the essential flexibility inherent in the style of this folk music; he has the good sense to avoid bogging a song down with heavy-handed musical setting; and, at the same time, he possesses the artistry necessary to *enhance* the song through an attractive, poetic, and nuanced musical environment in which the original material finds renewed life — goals not easily achieved.

This author's search for the performance materials for De Cormier's arrangements led him to the American state of Vermont, where De Cormier had gone into semi-retirement. In his phone conversation with De Cormier, he expressed his interest in performing his arrangements and asked where he could buy, or rent, the vocal scores and instrumental parts. With a hearty laugh, De Cormier said, "Those materials have been sitting in my storage closet for over forty years. I'd be *thrilled* if someone performed them!" Apparently, the arrangements had been written — and used — only for those three LP recordings, *but never performed live.* Fortunately, he took the materials home; but unfortunately (or, perhaps, *fortunately for us*), they lay in his storage cupboard for all that time.

Enchanted by the beauty and power of this music, and armed with the conviction that these songs *must* be heard, the author convinced De Cormier to allow him and Ms. Janes-Yaffé to give them a new life in the public light — on the global stage — and to help assure that this vibrant song repertoire, and the culture behind it, proudly takes its place among existing folksong arrangement repertoires. De Cormier agreed to give them exclusive performance and publication rights to his arrangements. In return, they entered into an agreement with him by which they would 1) perform the songs as widely as possible, 2) undertake a new commercial recording of the songs, and 3) arrange for the publication of the songs in the original voice-plus-instrumental-ensemble version (one to ten instruments, depending on the song) and in reduced versions for (a) voice and piano and (b) voice, violin, and piano. This was the genesis of *The Yiddish Folksong Project*.

The Questions of Style and Authenticity

It is only natural to be concerned about matters of style when preparing song interpretations, and particularly about the question of 'authenticity' when approaching folksong-based material. In the case of Yiddish-language folk song, such considerations are compounded and complicated by the fact that they generate continuous — and often heated — debate amongst scholars and practitioners. That debate is, by all indications, infused with very strong personal cultural identification, familial history, and the inherited regional cultural practices and differences in spoken dialects owing to the historical movement and diffusion of Jewish populations over the centuries and across the globe.

At a certain point, however, it became clear to us that the achievement of *literal* authenticity was a futile goal. Is it not impossible to perform early music in a truly authentic manner, unless we have audio documentation of the author's performance intentions? In fact, once one gets beyond the framework in which a song was originally created, once the lullaby improvised by a mother who sings over her baby's cradle gets passed to the woman next door, or moves on to another village, or to another country, or is passed down to another generation, *and it was not recorded at the moment of creation*, literal authenticity is lost. As soon as a song moves from one body to another body, any claim of authenticity must necessarily be put into question.

The critical question, it seems to this author, is *does it really matter*? It is certainly true that one should do a 'background check' on every song that one intends to sing in public; one should immerse oneself fully in the sentiment, atmosphere, and aesthetic of each song; and one should try to become an inhabitant of the world in which each song resides. But have audiences really enjoyed the songs of composers like Schubert, Schumann, Brahms, Tchaikovsky, Fauré, Debussy, and others, any less just because we have not had recordings of those composers performing their own songs, thereby enabling us to give so-called 'historically-informed' performances?

It is our proposition that 'authenticity' can only be *imagined* based on whatever knowledge is available relating to the historical and cultural realities of the time of the work's creation. And even with that, what does one do with an *anonymous* song, where one doesn't even know when, where, or how the melody and text came into being? This is not the music of a German people in a German land, or a Chinese people in a Chinese land. This is the music of millions of Jewish people living in many different lands across the globe; music that organically absorbed, digested, and integrated the musical environment in which it found itself; music that was transmitted across borders, and even across oceans.

The language

Mention has been made of the original LP recordings by Martha Schlamme and Netanya Davrath. Each of them pronounced Yiddish differently because they came from different parts of the world, one from Western Europe, one from Eastern Europe. When Schlamme sings *Rozhinkes mit mandlen*, it is different than when Davrath sings it. So, which one is 'historically informed'? Which one is 'authentic'? The matter of Yiddish pronunciation seems to elicit such strong proprietary feelings, that it takes on an almost litigious fervour. Ms. Janes-Yaffé once did a performance of these songs in Brooklyn, New York, and, as always, the printed programme contained translations of all the Yiddish song texts. After the performance, an elderly gentleman appeared in the 'green room' with his programme in hand and all the Yiddish texts marked up in red ink. He claimed that the Yiddish that had been sung was not authentic *because it was not the Yiddish he had learned from his parents*. (N.B. Ms. Janes-Yaffé was using the YIVO – Yidisher Visnshaftlikher Institut – 'Standard Yiddish Pronunciation' in her performance).

Thus, in reality, only the melody and text of the songs can be said to (possibly) have *any* measure of authenticity. Beyond that, the lack of specificity with regard to the context in which they were originally created, the 'X Factor' of the pronunciation, the nature of the arrangements, and the vocal style of the performer who sings the songs — all these things must be taken into account when the singer fashions her interpretations. For this reason, one would be justifiably skeptical when terms like 'traditional', 'authentic', and 'historically-informed' are used in a cavalier manner and without an accompanying disclaimer. One would justifiably be bothered by statements such as the one

Folksong Arrangement
and Dissemination, 'The
Yiddish Folksong Project',
and the Questions of
Style and Authenticity
(Continued)

that came from the famous harpsichordist Wanda Landowska when she said, "You play Bach your way, and I'll play him *his* way." It goes without saying that Ms. Landowska could not possibly have known how Bach played his own music; her only option would have been to *imagine* it based on the due diligence of her study.

So, where does this leave the performers, those trying to decide on an interpretive approach to these songs? Although all musicological considerations in the area of Yiddish are significant — and they certainly have been explored by experts in the field and documented both in writing and archival recordings — they are only partially of importance within the framework of folksong arrangement performance. Why? Because in the end, if the Yiddish Folksong Project team didn't hold the belief that there was some enduring universality inherent in those songs — outside of their original cultural, historical, musical context, like every other body of great song literature — there would be no need to take them on as a project; we would never have embarked on what was essentially a significant experiment in the communicative power of these songs on the global stage. And it is precisely that conviction that is at the core of this project.

The Yiddish Language

Yiddish is the thousand-year-old language of *Ashkenazi* (European) Jews. Unlike most languages, which are spoken by the residents of a particular area or by members of a particular nationality, Yiddish — at the height of its usage — was spoken by millions of Jews of different nationalities all across the globe.

The matter of the origins of Yiddish is a controversial one. Even today, in spite of extensive scholarship on the subject, and as recently as Alexander Beider's 2015 *The Origins of Yiddish Dialects*, the common wisdom emanating from Max Weinreich's *History of the Yiddish Language* (1973) is being challenged. Weinreich and other Jewish-oriented 'millennialists' often view Yiddish as a separate language from the beginning of Jewish settlement in German lands in the ninth and tenth centuries. Beider and others fail to find convincing evidence of this. They take more of the 'Germanist' approach and argue that the language branched off from Early New High German at the end of the fifteenth century. Whatever the case, Yiddish was based on a mixture of (a) the existing Middle High German dialects and (b) the immigrants' own Jewish-French (known as *Western La'az*), Jewish-Italian (known as *Southern La'az*), and Hebrew. Written in Hebrew characters, Yiddish initially served as a Jewish-conversational *auxiliary* to Hebrew, which was solely the language of prayer, ritual, and scholarly and legal commentaries.

In the Late Middle Ages (ca. 1250-1500), many Jews migrated eastward from Western Europe to escape persecution. The exposure of Yiddish to the Slavic languages (Czech, Polish, Lithuanian, etc.) transformed it from a Germanic dialect to what is today referred to as a 'fusion language'. By the sixteenth century, Eastern Europe had become the center of world Jewry. Eventually, Yiddish culture was so rich in the East that the language had few detractors amongst Jews and was seen as being more central to Jewish identity than it was in the West, where Jews had begun to enter secular schools, where the language of instruction was the vernacular (e.g., German, French, Dutch, etc.), and to work in professions that required a knowledge of secular language in order to communicate with non-Jews. Many of these western Jews looked down on Yiddish as a product of the insular, 'unworldly' Jewish *shtetl* (rural village) of the East. A division began to develop between the 'Eastern Yiddish' of those living in Slavic lands and the 'Western Yiddish' of those who had remained in the West. The fact remains, however, that around eighty percent of Yiddish vocabulary is derived from the Germanic, fifteen percent from the Hebraic and Aramaic, and five percent from the Slavic, Latin, and Romance languages.

Before the Holocaust, there were an estimated *eleven million* speakers of Yiddish; two out of three Jews

The Yiddish Language
(Continued)

in the world spoke the language. On the eve of World War II, there were sixty Yiddish daily newspapers and 300-400 daily periodicals in thirty different countries. The persecutions and the genocide exacted by the Nazi-regime and its accomplice nations between 1933 and 1945 led to the annihilation of a vast number of Yiddish speakers, dealing an almost lethal blow to the language. It is estimated that there are only about *two million* speakers left, most of whom no longer use Yiddish as their primary, everyday language. In the United States and Britain most post-Holocaust Yiddish speakers tended not to pass the language to their children, who assimilated and spoke English. The exceptions to this are, for example, some ultra-orthodox Jewish communities in the USA (e.g., New York, New Jersey), the UK (e.g., London, Manchester, Leeds), France (Paris), Belgium (Antwerp), and Canada (Montréal). Thus, Yiddish is considered a Germanic 'folk' language and an endangered 'heritage language'.

In recent years, however, as a result of renewed interest in Ashkenazi culture, Yiddish language courses are being taught in many Jewish cultural organizations, and many universities around the world offer courses — and even degree programs — in Yiddish linguistics. Even German language linguists are learning Yiddish due to the fact that the development of modern German is inextricably linked to the medieval versions of it, versions that today are manifest only in Yiddish. There are hundreds of newspapers, magazines, radio programs, and websites in Yiddish worldwide. Moreover, Yiddish is receiving attention from the *non-Jewish* scholarly community as a real language, and not as the 'corrupted tongue' that it was considered throughout history. One example of this is the fact that the Yiddish-language author Isaac Bashevis Singer, born in Poland in 1902 and emigrated to the USA in 1935, was awarded the Nobel Prize for Literature in 1978.

Yiddish is a highly plastic and assimilative language, rich in idioms, and possessing remarkable freshness, pithiness, and pungency. Since it was spoken by ordinary people rather than by scholars, its vocabulary is weak in abstractions and has few items descriptive of nature. Yet, Yiddish has a wealth of words descriptive of character and of relations among people. It also makes liberal use of diminutives and terms of endearment; it has a variety of expletives; and the use of proverbs is considerable (as can be see throughout this volume). These qualities and usages give Yiddish a uniquely warm and personal flavor. It is a language rich in irony, as exemplified by the following proverb on economic theory: 'Rich and poor both lie *in* the ground together, but *on* the ground the rich lie more comfortably'.

Eight Reasons to Keep the Yiddish Language Alive

(in 'countdown' order)

No. 8: Yiddish is the best way to understand the soul of the Jewish people.

No. 7: Yiddish allows you to communicate with the past, the dead, as well as the living.

No. 6: Yiddish is the way to enter the doors of a magnificent literature and culture.

No. 5: Yiddish brings sacred concepts and beautiful traditions down to earth and makes them comprehensible.

No. 4: Yiddish has profound insights and wisdom that lose a great deal of their power in translation.

No. 3: Yiddish teaches an optimistic vision that allows us to view the world with joy and with hope.

No. 2: Yiddish teaches us how to laugh more loudly and how to weep with more feeling.

No. 1: To know Yiddish is to become an artist with words and a master at describing the foibles, the quirks, and the strengths of human character.

— **Rabbi Benjamin Blech**

Yiddish Pronunciation Guide

The chart below is based on 'Standard Yiddish', the literary Yiddish established by YIVO (Yidisher Visnshaftlikher Institut), taught in Yiddish schools and university courses, and conceived as a guide for *spoken* Yiddish.

In our chart, YIVO's guidelines are amended to include considerations particular to *sung Yiddish*. For example:

•   For each vowel and consonant listed below, the corresponding IPA (International Phonetic Alphabet) symbol is given. These symbols will combine to form the complete IPA transliterations given for each individual song text in this anthology.

•   The unstressed 'e' (IPA symbol [ɜ]) is, *in sung Yiddish*, preferable to the common *schwa* [ə].

VOWELS
(NOTE: Yiddish vowels are generally of medium length, as distinguished from the long and short vowels in English and German).

Transliteration Letter	Closest English Equivalent	IPA Symbol	Yiddish Examples
a	Close to the 'a' in 'father'	[a]	ale, baruf
e (stressed)	Open 'e' as in 'bet'	[ɛ]	esn, avek
e (unstressed)	Midway between the *schwa* [ə], as in 'ever' or 'celebrate', and the open 'e' as in 'bet'	[ɜ]	libe, zingen
i (closed)	Like the 'ee' in 'need'	[i]	gis, papir
i (open)	Like the 'i' in 'pit'	[ɪ]	iz, vinter, kloyznik
o (closed)	Close to the 'o' in 'obey'	[o]	yorn
o (open)	Close to the 'ough' in 'ought'	[ɔ]	vos, sholem
u (closed; final vowel in a single-syllable word)	Like the 'oo' in 'goose'	[u]	du, vu
u (open)	Like the 'u' in 'put'	[ʊ]	undz, genug

SEMIVOWEL

Transliteration Letter	Closest English Equivalent	IPA Symbol	Yiddish Examples
y (as the initial consonant of a syllable)	Like the 'y' in 'yellow'	[j]	yiddish, faryosemte

DIPHTHONGS

Transliteration Letters	Closest English Equivalent	IPA Symbol	Yiddish Examples
ay	Like the 'y' in 'dry' and 'fine'	[aɪ]	ayer, zayn
ey	Like the 'ay' in 'say' and 'pain'	[ɛɪ]	eybig, freylekh
oy	Like the 'oy' in 'toy' and 'loin'	[ɔɪ]	oyfhern, azoy

SPECIAL CONSONANT SOUNDS

Transliteration Letters	Closest English Equivalent	IPA Symbol	Yiddish Examples
kh	A *slightly* stronger guttural than the 'ch' in 'Bach'	[x]	kheyder, makhn, aykh
n, in combination with 'g' or 'k'	Nasalized, like the 'n' in 'sing' and 'Thinker'	[ŋ]	zingen, benken (Note: In Yiddish, the 'g' and 'k' are *always* articulated when followed by an 'e')
r	Always flipped; never silent	[ɾ]	broyt, baruf, tayer
sh	Like the 'sh' in 'shine'	[ʃ]	sheyn, farshemen, Moyshe
tsh	Like the 'ch' in 'check'	[tʃ]	tshiri, khotsh
zh	Like the 's' in 'measure'	[ʒ]	zhe, rozhinkes, huzhen

CONSONANTS NOT LISTED ABOVE:
- The following single consonants are pronounced exactly as in English (when not part of one of the 'Special Consonant Sounds' listed above):
  b, d, f, h, k, l, m, n, p, s, t, v, z

- The following consonants do not exist in Yiddish transliteration:
  c, j, q, w, x

REGARDING THE PRONUNCIATION of 'b', 'd', and 'g':
- The consonants 'b', 'd', and 'g' are *always* pronounced as *voiced* consonants in Yiddish — no matter where they occur in the word.

- This demands special attention when they occur at the end of a word. The consonants 'b', 'd', and 'g' should *never* be modified to the *unvoiced* consonants 'p', 't', or 'k' (respectively) as they would be in German.

- Please see the next article in this anthology: 'Yiddish in Comparison with GermanGerman: Some Cautionary Remarks Regarding Pronunciation'.

REGARDING SYLLABLES AND THEIR STRESS
- In the IPA transliterations provided before each song, the division of syllables is shown by a separating dot, e.g.:

  [hu.ʒɛn]

- In general, two-syllable words have their stress on the *first* of those syllables. Where this is not the case — and in the case of words with more than two syllables — a stress mark (') has been placed *before* the accented syllable, e.g.:

  [faɾ.'ʃɛ.mɛn]

Yiddish in Comparison with German: Some Cautionary Remarks Regarding Pronunciation

The challenge

Every language presents its own unique set of pronunciation challenges. In the case of Yiddish, a particular challenge arises in that Yiddish is a language of Germanic origin (Middle High German, to be specific). Despite the metamorphosis that the Yiddish language experienced in the course of its evolution, German vocabulary remains at its core; in fact, approximately eighty percent of its vocabulary is rooted in German. At first, this would appear to be a 'plus' to any singer already familiar with the German language. However, experience has shown that while a familiarity with German can, admittedly, afford the singer 'a foot in the door', it is also fraught with pitfalls.

At the outset, it is important for the singer to remember that *Yiddish is not German*. These are two different languages, and they are manifestations of two different cultures. However, the singer who possesses a knowledge of German can easily find herself, almost without noticing, defaulting to *Hochdeutsch* ('High German') pronunciation. *Hochdeutsch* is the contemporary language of German that every student of German, and every singer of classical music, learns today. There is just enough similarity between *Hochdeutsch* and Yiddish words of Germanic origin to simultaneously *comfort* and to *frustrate* even the most experienced professional singer.

In this volume, the singer will be reading a standard Latin-alphabet transliteration (that is, a Romanization) of Yiddish (traditionally in Hebrew alphabet). It will be noticed that in these transliterations the spelling of Yiddish words of Germanic origin *does* differ from the *Hochdeutsch* spelling. This is a direct result of the differences in pronunciation of the two languages. Nonetheless, there will be a strong tendency for a German-speaking/singing performer to deliver Germanic Yiddish words with a *Hochdeutsch* pronunciation; that is, to make the following errors, for example:

* to say 'klar' (Ger.) instead of 'klor' (Yid.)
* to say 'auf' (Ger.) instead of 'oyf' or 'af' (Yid.)
* to say 'kein' (Ger.) instead of 'keyn' (Yid.)
* to say 'teuer' (Ger.) instead of 'tayer' (Yid.)
* to use the 'ich-Laut' [ç] (as in the German 'Be<u>ch</u>er') instead of the [x] in 'be<u>kh</u>er'

Such tendencies can be irresistible and must be avoided at all costs. The singer must, therefore, invest additional, and very conscious, effort in weaning herself off the automatic (albeit understandable) defaulting to *Hochdeutsch* pronunciation.

Yiddish in Comparison
with German:
Some Cautionary
Remarks Regarding
Pronunciation
(Continued)

The silver lining

The silver lining in this scenario is the fact that the standardization of Yiddish language transliteration is widely accepted, and it is a 'what-you-see-is-what-you-get' proposition; *it is virtually without irregularities*. That is: learn the sounds of the vowels and consonants (and the consonant groups) by way of the IPA (International Phonetic Alphabet), and you are on your way to having a command of Yiddish lyric diction. (More on this matter will be found on subsequent pages of this volume.)

The nitty-gritty: vowels, diphthongs, and consonants

In Yiddish vocabulary of Germanic origin, the differences between *Hochdeutsch* and Standard Yiddish pronunciation are mainly in the vowels and diphthongs. For example:

- The German long [a:] as in 'V<u>a</u>ter' ('f<u>a</u>ther') is [ɔ] in Yiddish 'f<u>o</u>ter'.

- The German long [e:] and long [o:], are diphthongs in Yiddish: *ey* and *oy*.

- As with certain other Germanic languages, Yiddish lacks the German front-rounded umlaut vowels *ö* [ø] and *ü* [y]. They are replaced in Yiddish by [ɛɪ] and [i] respectively.

- In the case of diphthongs, too, Yiddish and German have developed differently from their roots in Middle High German. As *Hochdeutsch* evolved, it combined the Middle High German diphthong ei [ei] (as in '<u>ei</u>nen' [einən]) and the long vowel *î* [i:] (as in 'm<u>î</u>n' [min]) into one diphthong *ei* [ɑe], hence the *Hochdeutsch* 'einen' [ɑenən] and 'mein' [mɑen]. In Yiddish, however, the Middle High German *ei* and *î* remained two different sounds but became *ey* [ɛɪ], as in '<u>ey</u>nen', and *ay* [aɪ], as in 'm<u>ay</u>n'.

  - The German [ao] (as in 'k<u>au</u>fen') corresponds to the Yiddish [ɔɪ] (as in 'k<u>oy</u>fn'). Finally, the German [ɔø] (as in 'D<u>eu</u>tsch') corresponds to [aɪ] in Yiddish (in 'd<u>ay</u>tsh').

Notable consonantal differences between German and Yiddish include:

- Alteration of the German initial 'affricate' *pf* (as in 'Pfund') to *f* (as in the Yiddish 'funt')

- Alteration of the German final affricate *pf* (as in 'Kopf') to *p* (as in the Yiddish 'kop')

Important Reminders:

• The consonants 'b', 'd', and 'g' are *always* pronounced as voiced consonants in Yiddish — no matter where they occur in the word. This demands special attention when they occur at the end of a word: the consonants 'b', 'd', and 'g' should *never* be modified to the *unvoiced* consonants 'p', 't', or 'k', respectively — as they would be in German.

• Many Yiddish words end with a *syllabic consonant*. That is, the final syllable in these words has no vowel, only 'voiced consonants'. The final consonant is to be sustained for the duration of the note under which it stands (for example, '*ma.khn*', '*ble.tl*', '*bin.dn*', '*va. serl*'). It is imperative that the singer does not insert a vowel between these consonants. One must elide one consonant directly to the next. Any insertion of a vowel — despite any argument made regarding projection of vocal sound in performance — would be antithetical to an accurate realization of a Yiddish text, and it must be avoided at all costs. The singer may find this counter to everything they've learned. However, with practice, it can be mastered, and it is a critical component of idiomatic Yiddish singing diction.

On the following page will be found a chart comparing German and Yiddish vowels and diphthongs

German and Yiddish Vowels and Diphthongs in Comparison

VOWELS	German	=	Yiddish
Vowel:	closed *a* [ɑː]	=	o [ɔ]
Example:	V*a*ter, s*a*gen	=	f*o*ter, z*o*gn
Vowel:	open *a* [a]	=	o [ɔ]
Example:	d*a*s	=	d*o*s
	or		
	open *a* [a]	=	a [a]
	l*a*chen	=	l*a*khn
Vowel:	closed *e* or *ä* [eː]	=	ey [ɛɪ]
Example:	*E*sel or n*ä*hen	=	*e*yzl, n*e*yen
Vowel:	open *e* or *ä* [ɛ]	=	e [ɛ]
Example:	M*e*nsch, kr*ä*chzen	=	m*e*ntsh, kr*e*khtsn
Vowel:	closed *i* [i]	=	i [i]
Example:	l*i*egen, ~~dir~~	=	l*i*gn, ~~dir~~
Vowel:	open *i* [ɪ]	=	i [ɪ]
Example:	m*i*t, W*i*nd	=	m*i*t, v*i*nt
Vowel:	closed *o* [oː]	=	oy [ɔɪ]
Example:	h*o*ch, sch*o*n	=	h*oy*kh, sh*oy*n
Vowel:	open *o* [ɔ]	=	o [ɔ]
Example:	K*o*pf, s*o*llen	=	k*o*p, z*o*ln
Vowel:	closed *u* [u]	=	u [u]
Example:	z*u*, d*u*	=	ts*u*, d*u*
Vowel:	open *u* [ʊ]	=	u [ʊ]
Example:	B*u*tter, *u*nd	=	p*u*ter, *u*n
Vowel:	closed *ö* [øː]	=	ey [ɛɪ]
Example:	sch*ö*n	=	sh*ey*n
Vowel:	open *ö* [œ]	=	e [ɛ]
Example:	k*ö*nnen, K*ö*pfe	=	k*e*nen, k*e*p
Vowel:	closed *ü* [yː]	=	i [i]
Example:	gr*ü*n	=	gr*i*n
Vowel:	open *ü* [ʏ]	=	i [ɪ]
Example:	Br*ü*cke, f*ü*nf	=	br*i*k, f*i*nf
Vowel:	The 'schwa': *e* [ə]	=	e [ɜ]
Example:	g*e*denken, Lieb*e*	=	zh*e*, melam*e*d

DIPHTHONGS	German		=	Yiddish		
Diphthong:	*ei* [ɑe]	**or** *ai* [ɑe]	=	ey [ɛɪ]	**or**	ay [aɪ]
Example:	Fl*ei*sch	**or** M*ai*	=	fl*ey*sh		m*ay*n
Diphthong:	*au* [ɑo]		=	oy [ɔɪ]		
Example:	*au*ch, l*au*fen		=	*oy*kh, l*oy*fn		
Diphthong:	*eu* [ɔø]		=	ay [aɪ]		
Example:	D*eu*tsch		=	d*ay*tsh		

Sources

The information on the preceding pages, and the song descriptions on the following pages, are based in part on sources including the following:

Anon. (n.d.) A History of Yiddish. University of California at Los Angeles [online] available on <https://germanic.ucla.edu/about-us/germanic-languages/yiddish>

Avey, T. (n.d.) 'Passover'. *Tori Avey, Every Day Inspired by the Past* [online] available on https://toriavey.com/what-is-passover

Beregovski, M. (1962) *Evreiskie narodnye pesni*. Moscow: Sovetskii Kompositor

Blech, Rabbi M. (2000) *The Complete Idiot's Guide to Learning Yiddish*. Indianapolis: Alpha Books

Burko, A. (2016) '*The New Yiddish Dialectology: A Review of Alexander Beider's The Origins of Yiddish Dialects*', in *In geveb: A Journal of Yiddish Studies* [online] available from <ingeveb.org/articles/new-yiddish-dialectology>

Katz, D. (2010) 'Yiddish: Language'. YIVO *Encyclopedia of Jews in Eastern Europe* [online] available on <http://yivoencyclopedia.org/article.aspx/Language/Yiddish>

Kleine, A. (2003) 'Standard Yiddish'. *Journal of the International Phonetic Association*, 33: 261-265

Loeffler, J. (2010-2019) 'The Nigun'. *My Jewish Learning* [online] available on https://www.myjewishlearning.com/article/the-nigun

Mlotek, C. and Slobin, M. (2007) *Yiddish Folksongs from the Ruth Rubin Archive*. Detroit: Wayne State University Press

Mlotek, E. and Gottlieb, M. (1983) *We Are Here*. New York: Workmen's Circle

Mlotek, E.G. and Mlotek, J. (1988) *Pearls of Yiddish Song*. New York: Workmen's Circle

Mlotek, E.G. and Mlotek, J. (1997) *Songs of Generations*. New York: Workmen's Circle

Mlotek, E.G. (2000) *Mir trogn a gezang*. 4th edn. New York: Workmen's Circle

Pasternak, V. (ed.) (1998) *The Yiddish Anthology: Classic Folksongs for Voice and Piano*. Owings Mills: Tara Publications

Schlamme, M. (1957) [Liner notes]. *Jewish Folk Songs, Volume 1* [LP]. New York: Vanguard Records

Schlamme, M. (1959) [Liner notes]. *Jewish Folk Songs, Volume 2* [LP]. New York: Vanguard Records

Weinberger, M. (2010) 'A Mystical Explanation of an old Jewish Folk Song'. *The Jewish Magazine* [online] available from <http://www.jewishmag.com/144mag/dona_dona/dona_dona.htm>

The Arrangements of Robert De Cormier

The Yiddish folk song was sung and disseminated primarily by the Jews of Eastern Europe. It constitutes a lyrical reflection of the thoughts, feelings, and experiences of a people. The songs shed light on religious and secular practices and customs, holidays, and celebrations and convey personal insights into daily life and historical events.

The eighteen songs that follow have been chosen for the breadth of their subject matter and sentiment, as well as for the richness of their musical expression. There are songs of celebration, riddle songs, love songs telling of the longing and separation of lovers, of unrequited love affairs, of disputes between good and evil inclinations, of existential contemplation, of personal or familial tragedies, and of pogroms; there are also songs of resistance against oppression, Bible-story-based 'cumulative' songs, ironical songs gently poking fun at the Chasidic movement, cradle songs, children's songs, and even drinking songs.

Robert De Cormier has left us a veritable treasure-trove of Yiddish folksong arrangements. With his unique blend of intellect, emotional intelligence, insight, artistry, capacity for nuance, inventiveness — and with impeccable craft — he has furthered and enriched the folksong arrangement repertoire immeasurably. And now, after sixty years, his arrangements are finally, and for the first time, handed over to you, the singer, or the voice student, or the voice teacher, or the coach, or the scholar, for your artistic fulfillment and your pleasure. May these arrangements enrich your lives and your repertoire, as they have ours.

The Yiddish Folksong Project Team

THE
YIDDISH
FOLKSONG
PROJECT
ANTHOLOGY

The arrangements of Robert De Cormier

Volume I
18 Songs

'To life, to life, l'khayim!'
— Sung by **Tevye** in the musical *Fiddler on the Roof*

1
A dudele

This is a prayerful song, sung directly to God, and an example of the very personal relationship that the Jewish people have with God. When the singer calls out to God, she uses the familiar pronoun 'du'. In Yiddish, the word 'du' means 'you'. She sings, "Master of the World, I want to sing a song to *you*." The theme of the song, God's presence in all places, at all times, and in all events, is a theme typical of the Jewish High Holy Days of Rosh Hashanah (Jewish New Year) and Yom Kippur (Day of Atonement).

It has been suggested that the title is a play on the word 'du', associating it with 'doodling' — that is, a melody and lyric structure that has no strict form, but rather 'doodles' around. It might have been composed spontaneously, or by combining several thoughts and feelings the author had had previously. Still others have suggested also that there is an allusion to the 'dudka', the Russian name for a shepherd's musical pipe. Whatever the case, the song is a Chasidic* 'classic', a meditation on the omnipresence and intimate nearness of God.

* Chasidic: This refers to the followers of the ultra-orthodox Chasidic form of Judaism, characterized by religious zeal and a spirit of prayer, joy, and charity. Song and dance have been important values of the Chasidic movement since its beginnings in the eighteenth century.

1
A dudele

a du.dʒ.lə
A dudele
A song

Attributed to Levi Yitskhok of Berditchev (1740-1809)

TEXT:
- IPA Transliteration
- **Sung Text**
- Word-for-Word Translation

| IDIOMATIC TRANSLATION |

ɹɪ.ˈbɔɪ.nɔɪ ʃɛl ʔɔɪ.ˈlɔm
Riboynoy shel oylom,
Master of the world

dɪr

ɪx vɛl dir ʔa ˈdu.dʒ.lə zɪŋ.gən
Ikh vel dir a dudele zingen.
I want (to)you a song sing

du du
Du du
You you

> Master of the world,
> I want to sing a song to you:
> You, You…

a.jɛɪ ʔɛm.ˈtsɔ.ɛ.xɔ
Ayey emtzo'ekho?
Where can I find you

vɛ.ˈʔa.jɛɪ lɔɪ ʔɛm.ˈtsɔ.ɛ.xɔ
V'ayey loy emtzo'ekho?
And where not can I find you

vu kɛn ʔɪx dɪx jɔ gɜ.ˈfɪ.nən
Vu ken ikh dikh yo gefinen?
Where can I you yes find

ʊn vu kɛn ʔɪx dɪx nɛ.dɜr gɜ.ˈfɪ.nən
Un vu ken ikh dikh neder gefinen?
And where can I you not find

du du
Du, du …
You you…

> Where am I to find you?
> Where am I not to find you?
> Where am I to find you?
> Where am I not to find you?
> You, you…

az vu ʔɪx gɛɪ du
Az vu ikh gey, du,
As wherever I go you

ʊn vu ʔɪx ʃtɛɪ du
Un' vu ikh shtey, du.
And wherever I stand you

ɹak du nɔr du vi.dɜr du ʔax du
Rak du, nor du, vider du, akh du.
Always you only you again you ah you

du du
Du, du…
You, you

> Wherever I go: You.
> And wherever I find myself: You.
> Always You, only You, again You, ah You.
> You, You…

ɪz ˈʔɛ.mɛt.sɜn gʊt du
Iz emetsen gut, du,
Is somebody good you

xɔ.ˈli.lə ʃlɛxt ʔaɪ aɪ aɪ du
Kholile schlekht, ay, ay, ay, du,
God forbid bad oh oh oh you

> When things go well: You.
> When, God forbid, things go badly: You.
> Ay, ay, ay, ay, You.
> You, You…

mɪz.ɾɔx du maɪ.ɾɛv du tsɔ.fn̩ du dɔ.ɾɛm du
Mizrokh du, mairev, du, tzofn du, dorem du,
East   you west   you north you south   you

maɪ.lɔ   du ma.tɔ   du
Maylo   du, mato   du,
In the sky you on earth   you

'u.mɛ.tʊm   ʔɪz nɔɾ du du
umetum   iz nor du, du,
everywhere is only you you

East: You, West: You, North: You, South: You.
In the heavens: You,
On earth: You, everywhere: You.
You, You…

vu   ʔɪx kɛɾ mɪx
Vu   ikh ker mikh,
Where I   turn myself

vu   ʔɪx zɛ mɪx du du
vu   ikh ze mikh, du, du!
where I   see myself you you

Wherever I turn, wherever I find myself: You, You!

1
A dudele

Attributed to
Levi Yitskhok of Berditchev (1740-1809)

Arrangement by Robert De Cormier
(piano reduction by John Yaffé)

Recitativo

Ri - boy - noy shel oy - lom, ri - boy - noy shel oy - lom, ri -
boy - noy shel oy - lom, ri - boy - noy shel oy - lom.
Ri - boy - noy shel oy - lom, ikh vel dir a du - de - le zin - gen

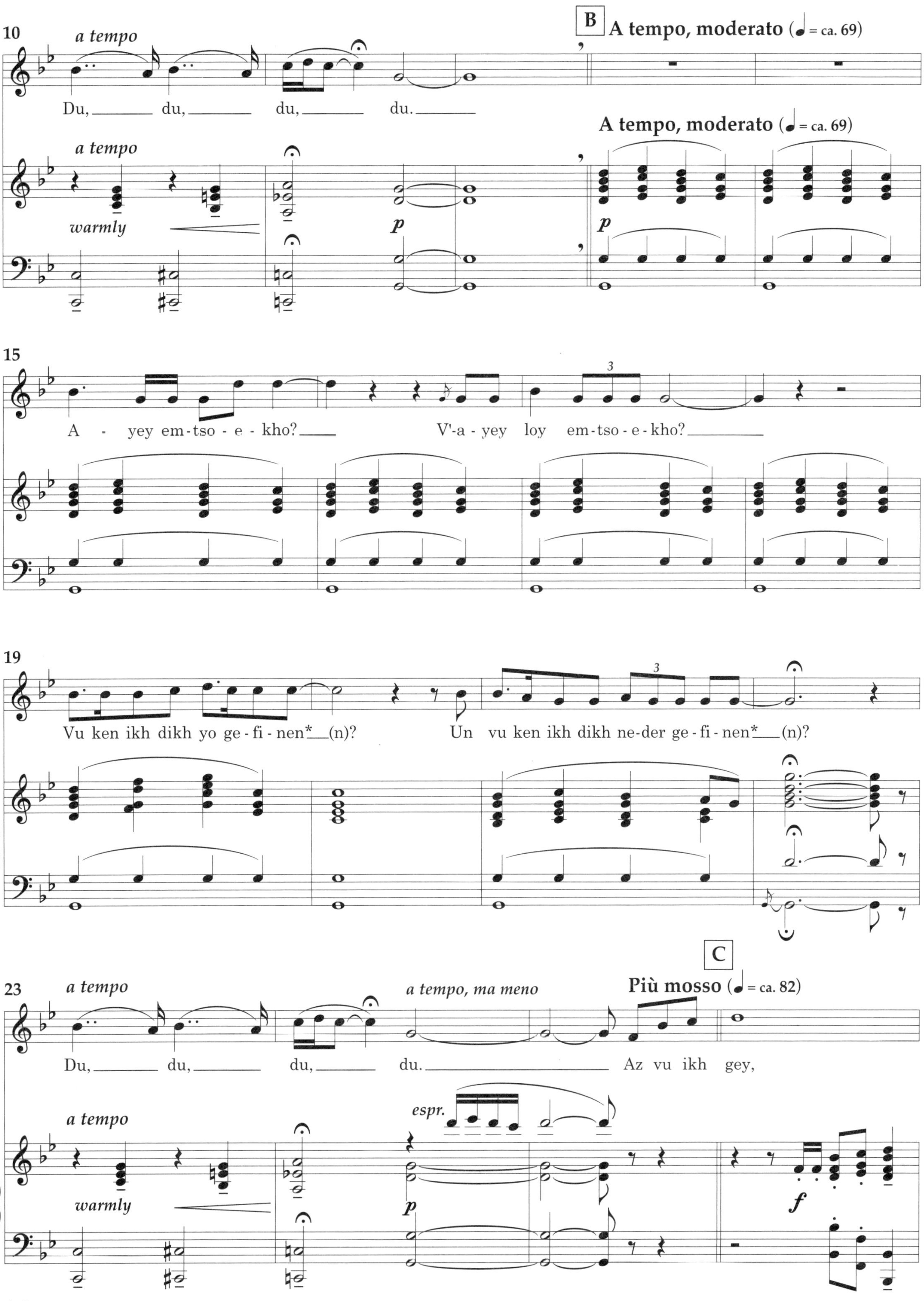

* Go to 'n' immediately and sustain.

27
du, un vu ikh shtey, du. Rak du, nor du,
mf
f
mf
31
rall.
a tempo, ma meno
a tempo
vi - der du, akh du. Du, du, du. du.
warmly
p
espr.
D
35
freely, come un recitativo
Iz e - met - sen gut, du, kho - li - le schlekht, ay, ay, ay,
p
col canto
una corda
39
du, ay du du du, du du du du du du du du.

42
E
A tempo, moderato, but rhythmic (♩ = 80-84)
Miz-rokh du, may-rev, du, tso-fn du, do-rem du, du, du, du, du, du, du, du, du,
A tempo, moderato, but rhythmic (♩ = 80-84)
mf firmly
due corde
45
du.
May-lo du, ma-to du, u-me-tum iz nor du,
espr.
48
du, du, du, du, du, du, du, du,
col canto
p
F
Grandly (♩ = ca. 66)
du, du, du, du, du, du, du, du, du.
mf
52
p
f
Vu ikh ker mikh, vu ikh ze mikh, du, du!
p col canto
p
gl.
sfz

*'When you put a bird in a cage, you don't
know whether it's laughing or crying'*
*('Az men zetst a feygele in shtaygele arayn,
veys men nit tsi lakht es tsi veynt es')*

– Yiddish proverb

2
A nign
(or 'Tshiri-bim')

A *nigun* is a form of Jewish (specificlly *Chasidic* Jewish) religious song or tune. It often contains repetitive sounds such as 'bim-bim-bam' or 'ay-ay-ay' instead of formal lyrics. Sometimes, Bible verses or quotes from other classical Jewish texts are sung repetitively to form a nigun. Some *nigunim* (plural) are sung as prayers of lament, while others may be joyous or victorious. Nigunim are central especially to worship in Chasidic Judaism, which evolved its own structured, soulful forms of nigunim to reflect the mystical joy of intense prayer. From the beginning of the Chasidic movement (in the eighteenth century), it was taught that song is an even greater form of spiritual expression than traditional prayer and that the nigun was a musical path to God that transcended the limitations of language itself.

2
A nign
(or **'Tshiri-bim'**)

a nı.gŋ
A nign
A Tune

Words: L. Magister (1887-1965)
Music: Lazar Weiner (1897-1982)

TEXT:
- IPA Transliteration
- **Sung Text**
- Word-for-Word Translation

IDIOMATIC TRANSLATION

ɪz a kab.tsŋ ʔa.ˈmɔl gɜ.ˈvɛ.zŋ
Iz a kabtsn amol gevezn,
Is a pauper once was

flɛgt ʔɛr nɔr mɪt gɔt zɪx kɾi.gŋ
flegt er nor mit got zikh krign.
Used to he only with God (—) quarrel

vʊn.dɜr ʔi.bɜr vʊn.dɜr hɔt mɪt ʔɪm gɜ.ˈtrɔ.fŋ
Vunder iber vunder hot mit im getrofn,
Wonders over wonders had with him met

vɛn ʔɛr hɔt gɜ.ˈzʊŋ.gɜn ʔɔt a.ˈzɔɪ mɪn nɪ.gŋ
Ven er hot gezungen ot azoy min nign:
When he had sung as such a tune

Once upon a time, there was a pauper,
He quarreled with no one (except God).
Wonders upon wonders would befall him
When he sang such a melody:

tʃɪ.ɾi bɪm bam bam tʃɪ.ɾi bɪ.ɾi bɪm bam
Tshiri bim bam bam, tshiri biri bim bam,
Tshiri bim bam bam tshiri biri bim bam

tʃɪ.ɾi bɪm bam bam ʔɔɪ tʃɪ.ɾi bɪ.ɾi bɪm bam
Tshiri bim bam bam, oy, tshiri biri bim bam,
Tshiri bim bam bam ah tshiri biri bim bam

tʃɪ.ɾi bɪm tʃɪ.ɾi bɪm tʃɪ.ɾi bɪm
Tshiri bim, tshiri bim, tshiri bim,
Tshiri bim tshiri bim tshiri bim

bɪm bam bam ba ba ba bam
Bim bam bam, ba ba ba bam.
Bim bam bam ba ba ba bam

Tshi-ri-bim-bam-bam
Tshi-ri-bi-ri-bim-bam,
Tshi-ri-bim-bam-bam,
Oy, tshi-ri-bi-ri-bim-bam,
Tshi-ri-bim, tshi-ri-bim, tshi-ri-bim,
Bim-bam-bam, ba-ba-ba-bam.

hɔt fʊn nɪ.gŋ zɪx vain gɜ.ˈgɔ.sŋ
Hot fun nign zikh vayn gegosn,
Had from tune itself wine flowed

hɔt ʔɛr zʊp nɔx zʊp gɜ.ˈʃlʊŋ.gɜn
Hot er zup nokh zup geshlungen.
Had he sip after sip swallowed

vʊn.dɜr ʔi.bɜr vʊn.dɜr hɔt mɪt ʔɪm gɜ.ˈtrɔ.fŋ
Vunder iber vunder hot mit im getrofn,
Wonders beyond wonder has with him met

vɛn ʔɛr hɔt gɜ.ˈzʊŋ.gɜn ʔɔt a.ˈzɔɪ gɜ.ˈzʊŋ.gɜn
Ven er hot gezungen ot azoy gezungen:
When he had sung like this sung

Wine flowed from the melody,
And he swallowed gulp after gulp.
Wonders upon wonders would befall him
When he sang a song like this:

tʃɪ.ɾi bɪm bam bam
Tshiri bim bam bam…(etc.)
Tshiri bim bam bam

Tshi-ri-bim-bam-bam…(etc.)

zɪŋgt dɛr jid ʔʊn sgɪst zɪx mɜ.'si.kɜs
Zingt der yid un s'gist zikh mesikes,
Sings the Jew and it flows itself sweetness

ɪz ɛr aʒ fʊn frɛɪd gɜ.'ʃprʊŋ.gɜn
Iz er azh fun freyd geshprungen.
Is he almost from joy leapt

vʊn.dɜr ʔi.bɜr vʊn.dɜr hɔt mɪt ʔim gɜ.'trɔ.fn̩
Vunder iber vunder hot mit im getrofn,
Wonder beyond wonder had with him met

vɛn ʔɛr hɔt gɜ.'zʊŋ.gɜn ʔɔt a.'zɔɪ gɜ.'zʊŋ.gɜn
Ven er hot gezungen ot azoy gezungen:
When he had sung as such sung

The Jew sings, and sweetness pours forth,
And he almost leaps for joy.
Wonders upon wonders would befall him
When he sang a song like this:

tʃɪ.ɾi bɪm bam bam
Tshiri bim bam bam…(etc.)
Tshiri bim bam bam

Tshi-ri-bim-bam-bam…(etc.)

2

A nign
(or 'Tshiri-bim')

Words by L. Magister (1887-1965)
Music by Lazar Weiner (1897-1982)

Arrangement by Robert De Cormier
(piano reduction by John Yaffé)

9
A tempo (♩= 66-78)
bam, tshi ri-bi-ri, bim, bam, tshi-ri-bim, bam,
A tempo (♩= 66-78)
11
bam, oy, tshi ri-bi-ri, bim, bam, tshi-ri-bim,
13
ritard.
pp
a tempo
tshi-ri-bim, tshi-ri-bim, bim, bam, bam, ba ba ba bam.
2. Hot fun
ritard.
a tempo
mp

16
C
Recitative
ni - gn zikh vayn - ge - go - sn, hot er zup nokh zup ge - shlun - gen; Vun - der i - ber
20
vun - der hot mit im ge - tro - fn ven er hot ge - zun - gen ot a - zoy ge
23
D
A tempo (♩= 66-78)
zun - gen: Tshi - ri - bim, bam, bam, tshi - ri - bi - ri, bim, bam, tshi - ri - bim, bam,
A tempo (♩= 66-78)
26
bam, oy, tshi - ri - bi - ri, bim, bam, tshi ri - bim,

tshi-ri-bim,___ tshi-ri-bim, bim, bam, bam, ba-ba-ba-bam.___

E **F** Recitative

3. Zingt der yid un s'gist zikh me - si-kes,___ iz er

azh fun freyd___ ge-shprun-gen;___ Vun-der i - ber vun-der___ hot mit im ge-

tro - fn ven er hot ge-zun-gen ot a-zoy___ ge-zun-gen:___ Tshi-ri-bim, bam,

A nign

bam,_____ tshi-ri-bi-ri, bim, bam,_____ tshi-ri-bim, bam,

bam, oy, tshi-ri-bi-ri, bim, bam,____ tshi-ri-bim,____

tshi-ri-bim,____ tshi-ri-bim, bim, bam, bam, ba-ba-ba-bam._____

'Man plans and God laughs'
('Mentsh trakht un Got lacht')

– Yiddish proverb

3
Aʒ der rebe zingt

The *Chasidic Jews* are a community of Jews that was formed in the mid-eighteenth century in the Ukraine and flourished particularly in the villages of Eastern Europe. Today, there are still pockets of Chasidic Jews around the world — around 130,000 households — principally in Israel, the U.S., Britain, and Canada. *Chasidism* is a mystical form of Judaism, characterized by religious zeal and a spirit of prayer, joy, and charity, and founded in reaction to the rigid academicism of *rabbinical Judaism.** Joy and its expression through song and dance have been important values of the Chasidic movement since its beginnings.

'Az der rebe zingt' is a mildly ironical song that depicts the joyful devotion of a group of Chasidics to their *rebe* (rabbi). Reverence and submission to the rebe are key tenets of Chasidism, as the rebe is considered a spiritual authority with whom the follower must bond to gain closeness to God.

There exist many variants of the verses of this song in different publications, where one can find the rebe eating, laughing, coughing, sneezing, standing, jumping, running — and even being silent.

rabbinical Judaism: The normative form of Judaism that developed after the fall of the Temple of Jerusalem (A.D. 70). Originating in the work of the Pharisaic rabbis, it was based on the legal and commentative literature in the Talmud, designed to control the interpretation of Jewish scripture, and it set up a mode of worship and a life discipline that were to be practiced by Jews worldwide down to modern times.

As der rebe zingt

3

az dɛɾ ɾɛ.bɜ zɪŋgt
Az der rebe zingt
When the rabbi sings

(Anonymous)

TEXT:
- IPA Transliteration
- **Sung Text**
- Word-for-Word Translation

IDIOMATIC TRANSLATION

ʊn ʔaz dɛɾ ɾɛ.bɜ zɪŋgt
Un az der rebe zingt,
And when the Rabbi sings

zɪŋ.gɜn ʔa.lɜ xa.'si.dɪm
Zingen ale khasidim,
Sing all(the) Chasidics

ja la la la la
Ya la la la la

When the Rabbi sings,
All the Chasidics sing:
Ya la la la la, ya la la la la —
All the Chasidics sing.

ʊn ʔaz dɛɾ ɾɛ.bɜ tantst
Un az der rebe tantst,
And when the Rabbi dances

tan.tsṇ ʔa.lɜ xa.'si.dɪm
Tantsn ale khasidim,
Dance all(the) Chasidics

tɾa ja ja ja ja
Tra ya ya ya ya

When the Rabbi dances,
All the Chasidics dance:
Tra ya ya ya ya, tra ya ya ya ya —
All the Chasidics dance.

ʊn ʔaz dɛɾ ɾɛ.bɜ vɛint
Un az der rebe veynt,
And when the Rabbi cries

vɛɪ.nɜn ʔa.lɜ xa.'si.dɪm
Veynen ale khasidim,
Cry all (the) Chasidics

ɔɪ ɔɪ ɔɪ ɔɪ ɔɪ
Oy oy oy oy oy

When the Rabbi cries,
All the Chasidics cry:
Oy oy oy oy oy, oy oy oy oy oy —
All the Chasidics cry.

ʊn ʔaz dɛɾ ɾɛ.bɜ laxt
Un az der rebe lacht,
And when the Rabbi laughs

la.xṇ ʔa.lɜ xa.'si.dɪm
Lachn ale khasidim,
Laugh all(the) Chasidics

ha ha ha ha ha
Ha ha ha ha ha

When the Rabbi laughs,
All the Chasidics laugh:
Ha ha ha ha ha, ha ha ha ha ha —
All the Chasidics laugh.

ʊn ʔaz dɛɾ ɾɛ.bɜ faɪft
Un az der rebe fayft,
And when the Rabbi whistles

faɪ.fṇ ʔa.lɜ xa.'si.dɪm
Fayfn ale khasidim
Whistle all(the) Chasidics

Pht pht pht pht pht
(Whistling in time)

When the Rabbi whistles,
All the Chasidics whistle:
Pht pht pht pht pht, pht pht pht pht pht —
All the Chasidics whistle.

3

As der rebe zingt

(Anonymous)

Arrangement by Robert De Cormier
(piano reduction by John Yaffé)

Moderato (♩ = 126)

allarg.

very broadly

poco più mosso, accel. poco a poco

cresc.

A Moderato (♩ = 92-100)

Un az der re - be zingt, un az der re - be zingt,

Moderato (♩ = 92-100)

Az der rebe zingt

Az der rebe zingt

* 'falling off the note, as with a sob

az der re - be veynt, vey - nen a - le kha - si - dim,

vey - nen a - le kha - si - dim, Oy oy oy oy oy, oy oy oy oy oy,

vey - nen a - le kha - si - - - dim, oy oy oy oy oy, oy oy oy oy oy,

vey - nen a - le kha - si - - - dim. Un az der re - be lakht, un az der re - be lakht, la - khn a - le kha - si - dim, la - khn a le kha-

si - - - dim: Ha_____ ha ha ha ha, ha_____ ha ha ha ha,

la - khn a - le kha - si - - - dim, ha_____ ha ha ha ha, ha_____

____ ha ha ha ha, la - khn a - le kha - si - dim.

Az der rebe zingt

28

Un az der re - be fayft, un az der re - be fayft, fay - fn a - le kha - si - - dim, fay - fn a - le kha - si - - dim: *(gefiffn)

* whistled

Az der rebe zingt

Az der rebe zingt

'Love thy neighbour, even if he plays the trombone'

– Yiddish proverb

4
Dona, dona, dona
(or 'Dos kelbl')

This metaphorical song was written by Sholom Secunda for Aaron Zeitlin's play *Esterke*, produced first in New York during the 1940-41 season. It subsequently became one of the most widely sung Yiddish songs, performed and recorded numerous times, including by internationally-renowned performers such as folk singers Joan Baez, Donovan, Theodore Bikel, and Chava Alberstein, French pop star Claude François, and opera singer Sumi Jo. Translations of the original Yiddish lyric have appeared in English, French, German, Indonesian, Italian, Japanese, Korean, Russian, Serbo-Croatian, Spanish, Swedish, and Vietnamese.

According to Mendel Weinberger:

> At first glance, this song seems like a light-hearted, somewhat sentimental dialogue between a farmer and his calf on the way to the slaughterhouse. The calf is sad because he is going to die, and the swallow is flying overhead, indifferent to the calf's plight. The farmer rebukes the calf, criticizing him for being one, and goading him into growing wings like the swallow, as if he could.
>
> The calf in the song represents the body, the seat of desire. The body and the animal soul that enlivens it desire pleasure, wealth, and honor. But like an animal, the body is a slave to these desires. The calf, bound and on the way to market to be slaughtered, is a metaphor for the body's journey towards death. The calf (i.e., the body) is mournful because it has become attached to life and pleasure and fears the unknown of the next world.
>
> The swallow winging swiftly through the sky represents the soul. The Divine Soul is a part of God's Being and is not bound by the material limitations of the physical world. It is free to soar in the spiritual realms high above the earthly one. The soul does not fear death for it is more at home in heaven than on earth.
>
> Why don't you have wings to fly with? Connect to your soul and transcend your physical limitations. Fly in the spiritual realm and feel your soul's power … if you treasure freedom, the freedom of the soul, then you will learn to transcend the limitations of the body and small mind, and you will understand your life from a higher perspective. You will be free.

There has been some speculation on the meaning of the word 'dona', but the most plausible definition is that it is simply a joyful exclamation used in Polish and other Slavic folk songs, often in formulas like 'oy, dana, dana!'.

4
Dona, dona, dona
(or "Dos kelbl")

dɔ.na dɔ.na dɔ.na dɔs kɛlbl̩
Dona dona dona (or **Dos kelbl**)
Dona dona dona

Words: Aaron Zeitlin (1898-1973)
Music: Sholom Secunda (1894-1974)

TEXT:
- IPA Transliteration
- **Sung Text**
- Word-for-Word Translation

IDIOMATIC TRANSLATION

ɔɪ.fn̩ fɔ.ɾl̩ ligt dɔs kɛl.bl̩
Oyfn forl ligt dos kelbl,
On the cart lies the calf

ligt gɜ'bʊn.dɜn mɪt ʔa ʃtɾɪk
Ligt gebunden mit a shtrik;
Lies bound with a rope

hɔɪx ʔɪn hɪ.ml̩ flit dɔs ʃvɛl.bl̩
Hoykh in himl flit dos shvelbl,
High in heaven flies the swallow

fɾɛɪt zɪx dɾɛɪt zɪx hɪn ʔʊn 'tsɾɪk
Freyt zikh dreyt zikh hin un ts'rik.
Enjoys himself turns himself forth and back

On a wagon there lies a little calf,
Lies bound with a rope;
High in the sky flies a swallow,
Joyfully circling back and forth.

laxt dɛɾ vɪnt ʔɪn kɔ.ɾn̩
Lakht der vint in korn,
Laughs the wind in wheatfield

laxt ʔʊn laxt ʔʊn laxt
Lakht un lakht un lakht;
Laughs and laughs and laughs

laxt ʔɛɾ ɔp ʔa tɔg ʔa gan.tsn̩
Lakht er op a tog a gantsn,
Laughs he off a day a whole one

mɪt ʔa hal.bɜɾ naxt
Mit a halber nakht.
With a half night

The wind laughs in the wheatfield,
Laughs and laughs and laughs;
It laughs for a whole day,
And half the night.

dɔ.na dɔ.na dɔ.na dɔ.na
Dona dona dona dona,
Dona dona dona dona

dɔ.na dɔ.na dɔ.na daɪ
Dona dona dona day;
Dona dona dona dai

Dona dona dona dona,
Dona dona dona dai;

ʃɾaɪt dɔs kɛl.bl̩ zɔgt dɛɾ pɔɪ.ɜɾ
Shrayt dos kelbl, zogt der poyer,
Screams the calf says the peasant

vɛɾ ʒɛ hɛɪst dɪx zaɪn ʔa kalb
"Ver zhe heist dikh zayn a kalb?
Who then named you to be a calf

vɔlst gɜ.'kɛɾt tsu zaɪn ʔa fɔɪ.gl̩
Volst gekert tsu zayn a foygl,
Want changed into being a bird

vɔlst gɜ.'kɛɾt tsu zaɪn ʔa ʃvalb
Volst gekert tsu zayn a shvalb!"
Want changed into being a swallow

The calf cries, and the farmer says,
"Who told you to be a calf?
You could be a bird,
You could be a swallow!"

laxt	dɛɾ	vɪnt	ʔɪn	kɔ.ɾn̩	
Lakht	**der**	**vint**	**in**	**korn**…(etc.)	
Laughs	the	wind	in	wheatfield	

The wind laughs in the wheatfield…(etc.)

dɔ.na	dɔ.na	dɔ.na	dɔ.na
Dona	**dona**	**dona**	**dona**…(etc.)
Dona	dona	dona	dona

Dona dona dona dona…(etc.)

bɪd.nɜ	kɛl.bɜɾ	tut	mɛn	bɪn.dn̩
Bidne	**kelber**	**tut**	**men**	**bindn,**
Poor	calves	does	one	bind

ʊn	mɛn	ʃlɛpt	zɛɪ	ʔʊn	mɛn	ʃɛxt
Un	**men**	**shlept**	**zey**	**un**	**men**	**shekht;**
And	one	drags	them	and	one	slaughters

vɛɾs	hɔt	fli.gl̩	flɪt	ʔa.ˈɾɔɪf	tsu
Ver's	**hot**	**fligl,**	**flit**	**aroyf**	**tsu,**
Who it	has	wings	flies	upward	to

ɪz	baɪ	kɛɪ.nɜm	nɪt	kɛɪn	knɛxt
Iz	**bay**	**keynem**	**nit**	**keyn**	**knekht.**
Is	by	no one	not	no	slave

Poor calves are bound
And dragged to slaughter;
Whoever has wings flies upwards
And is a slave to no one.

laxt	dɛɾ	vɪnt	ʔɪn	kɔ.ɾn̩	
Lakht	**der**	**vint**	**in**	**korn**…(etc.)	
Laughs	the	wind	in	wheatfield	

The wind laughs in the wheatfield…(etc.)

dɔ.na	dɔ.na	dɔ.na	dɔ.na
Dona	**dona**	**dona**	**dona**…(etc.)
Dona	dona	dona	dona

Dona dona dona dona…(etc.)

4

Dona, dona, dona
(or "Dos kelbl')

Words by Aaron Zeitlin (1898-1973)
Music by Sholom Secunda (1894-1974)

Arrangement by Robert De Cormier
(piano reduction by John Yaffé)

Allegretto (♩ = ca. 88)

Poco sostenuto (♩ = ca. 80)

1. Oy - fn fo - rl ligt dos kel - bl, ligt ge - bun - den___ mit a shtrik;
2. Shrayt dos kel - bl, zogt der po - yer, "Ver zhe heyst dikh___ zayn a kalb?

poco animato

poco rall.

Hoykh in hi - ml flit dos shvel - bl, freyt zikh, dreyt zikh___ hin un ts'rik.
Volst ge - kert tsu zayn a foy - gl, volst ge - kert tsu___ zayn a shvalb!"

9
Più mosso (♩ = ca. 92)
Lakht der vint in ko - rn, lakht un lakht un lakht; Lakht er op a
Più mosso (♩ = ca. 92)
f
p
f
14
B
Subito allegro (♩ = ca. 108)
tog a gan - tsn mit a hal - ber nakht. Do-na do-na do - na do - na,
Subito allegro (♩ = ca. 108)
p
mf
19
do-na do-na do - na day; Do-na do-na do - na do - na, do-na do-na do - na
24
L'istesso tempo
poco allarg.
day.
L'istesso tempo
poco allarg.
mf

C
29
Poco sostenuto (♩= ca. 80)
Bid - ne kel - ber tut men bin - dn, un men shlept zey un men shekht;
Poco sostenuto (♩= ca. 80)
p
33
poco animato
poco rall.
Ver's hot fli - gl, flit a - royf - tsu, iz bay key - nem nit keyn knekht.
poco animato
poco rall.
37
Più mosso (♩= ca. 92)
Lakht der vint in ko - rn, lakht un lakht un lakht;
Più mosso (♩= ca. 92)
f
p
41
Lakht er op a tog a gan - tsn mit a hal - ber nakht.
f
p

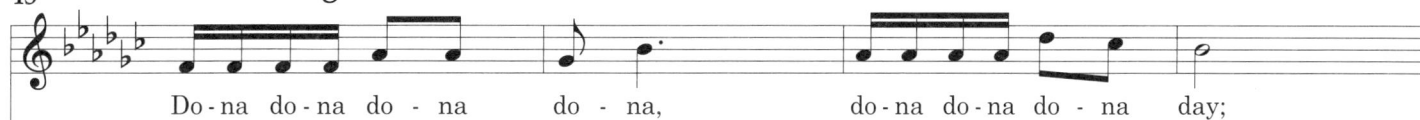

Do - na do - na do - na do - na, do - na do - na do - na day;

Do - na do - na do - na do - na, do - na do - na do - na day.___

Do - na do-na do - na do - na, do - na do-na do - na day;

Do - na do-na do - na do - na, do - na do-na do - na day.___

Dona dona dona

5
Freylekh

A *freylekh* is a common Chassidic, wordless dancing song intended for celebratory occasions. It is associated with a circle dance, is usually in the minor mode, typically played by a piano or accordion, in a duple metre, and with an 'oom-pah' beat.

The dance can involve any number of dancers who take each other by the hands or around the shoulders and dance in a circle. In the case of a great number of dancers, a smaller inner circle is formed. Often one or more dancers go out into the center of the circle; these may be particularly light and graceful, or they may do grotesque figures, and the tempos can vary from moderate to very quick. 'Freylekh' is the Yiddish word for 'festive', and the freylekh is a call to joy in life.

| 5
Freylekh | fɾɛɪ.lɜx
Freylekh
Joyful |
| | (Anonymous) |

TEXT:
- IPA Transliteration
- **Sung Text**
- Word-for-Word Translation

IDIOMATIC TRANSLATION

---

jʊm bʊm bʊm bʊm
Yum bum bum bum

jʊ dʊ daɪ di di dʊm dʊm
Yuh duh day di di dum dum…(etc.)

aɪ aɪ aɪ aɪ di di dʊm
Ay ay ay ay di di dum…(etc.)

Yum bum bum bum, yum bum bum bum,
Yuh duh dai di di dum dum…(etc.)
Ay ay ay ay di di dum,
Ay ay ay ay di di dum…(etc.)

fɾɛɪ.lɜx
Freylekh!
Joyful

Joyful!

5
Freylekh

(Anonymous)

Arrangement by Robert De Cormier
(piano reduction by John Yaffé)

Rubato

A **Larghetto** (♩ = ca. 58)

Rubato

espr. *mf*

Larghetto (♩ = ca. 58)

p

Yum bum bum bum, yum bum bum bum,

yuh duh day di di dum dum. Yum bum bum bum, yum bum bum bum, yuh duh day di di

dum. Yuh duh duh duh dum duh duh day di di dum dum, Ay di di di dum duh duh

12
B
day di di dum dum. Ay ay ay ay di di dum, ay ay ay ay di di dum.
17
Ay ay ay ay di di dum, ay ay ay ay di di dum. Ah,
rubato espr.
p
C
23
A tempo, ma un poco più (♩ = ca. 66)
ay ay ay di di, ay ay ay di di, ay ay yah di di di dum, ay ay yah di di di dum.
A tempo, ma un poco più (♩ = ca. 66)
mf
29
accelerando poco a poco
Ay ay ay ay ay ay ay ay ay; ay ay ay ay ay ay ay
accelerando poco a poco

yah duh dum di di dum.__ Yum bum bum bum, yum bum bum bum, yuh duh day di di

dum dum dum. Yum bum bum bum, yum bum bum bum, yuh duh day di di

dum. Yuh duh duh duh dum dum ay di di dum dum; Ay duh duh duh dum dum

ay di di dum dum. Ay ay ay ay di di dum,__ ay ay ay ay di di dum.

Freylekh

53
Ay ay ay ay di di dum, ay ay ay ay di di dum. Ah,
rubato espr.
p
58
F
Broader (♩ = ca. 76)
accelerando poco a poco
ay ay ay di di, ay ay ay di di, ay ay ay di di di dum,
Broader (♩ = ca. 76)
accelerando poco a poco
mf
63
ay ay ay di di di dum, Frey-lekh, ay ay ay! Ay yuh duh day di di
p
68
dum dum dum. Ay ay ay ay ay ay duh duh dum di di dum, hey!
cresc.

6
Lomir ale freylekh zayn

This indomitable song is a tribute to the people — many of them now advanced in years but still singing with youthful vigor — who have kept the tradition of Jewish choruses alive and strong. It has been sung at countless weddings and *barmitzvah** celebrations throughout the decades. Maddy Simon, a long-time social activist and the conductor of many amateur choruses throughout the New York area, recited the text of the song to us as we were preparing the notation of these arrangements. Additionally, she told us that this song is an ever-present part of the repertoire she teaches to young students and Jewish summer camp attendees.

*bar-mitzvah (or bat-mitzvah for girls): Hebrew for 'son / daughter of commandment'. When a Jewish boy / girl turns thirteen, they have all the rights and obligations of a Jewish adult, including the commandments of the Torah. From that date, they will participate in synagogue services and take their place in the Jewish community. Bar- / bat-mitzvah festivities typically include a celebratory meal with family, friends, and members of the community.

6
Lomir ale freylekh zayn

 lɔ.mɪr ʔa.lɜ fɾɛɪ.lɜx zaɪn
Lomir ale freylekh zayn
Let us all joyful be

(Anonymous)

TEXT:
- IPA Transliteration
- **Sung Text**
- Word-for-Word Translation

IDIOMATIC TRANSLATION

---

lɔ.mɪr ʔa.lɜ fɾɛɪ.lɜx zaɪn
Lomir ale freylekh zayn,
Let us all joyful be

lɔ.mɪr ʔa.lɜ zɪŋ.gɜn
lomir ale zingen.
let us all sing

zɪŋ.gɜn faɾ ʃɔ.lɜm
Zingen far sholem,
Sing for peace,

zɪŋ.gɜn faɾ bɾɔɪt
zingen far broyt;
sing for bread

bɔɪ.ɜn a mɔɾ.gn̩
Boyen a morgn
Build a tomorrow

ʔɔn has ʊn ɔn nɔɪt
on has un on noyt
without hate and without want

Let's all be joyful, let's all sing,
Sing for peace, sing for bread;
Build a tomorrow without hate
And without want.

6
Lomir ale freylekh zayn
(Anonymous)

Arrangement by Robert De Cormier
(piano reduction by John Yaffé)

Joyous, ecstatic (♩ = ca. 152)

Lo - mir a - le frey - lekh zayn,

lo - mir a - le zin - gen. Lo - mir a - le frey - lekh zayn, lo - mir a - le zin - gen.

Zin - gen far sho - lem, zin - gen far broyt; Bo - yen a mor - gn on has un on noyt.

Lyrics:
9. Zin - gen far sho - lem, zin - gen far broyt; Bo - yen a mor - gn on noyt,_____

13. bo - yen a mor - gn on noyt._____

16. **B** Day day day day day, day di day di day di; Day day day day day,

19. di di di day day. Zin - gen far broyt,

Lomir ale freylekh zayn

Lomir ale freylekh zayn

Zin - gen far sho - lem, zin - gen far broyt; Bo - yen a mor - gn on has un on noyt.

Zin - gen far sho - lem, zin - gen far broyt; Bo - yen a mor - gn on noyt,

bo - yen a mor - gn on noyt.

allarg. molto *a tempo*

Lomir ale freylekh zayn

'A man should live if only to satisfy his curiosity'

– Yiddish proverb

7
May-ko mashma lon

In this soliloquy, a destitute *yeshiva bokher* (rabbinical student) visualizes his life as he takes note of certain things around him. The rain reminds him that his boots are torn, and that he has no warm coat with which to face the winter; he sees nothing but wretchedness in his life; he has only a bench for a home and must depend on strangers for his meals; he has been wasting the *present* in futile agony, merely waiting for the *hereafter*.

7
May-ko mashma lon

maɪ kɔ maʃ.ma   lɔn
May- ko mashma   lon
What is the meaning of

Words: Abraham Reisen (1876-1953)
Music: (on a Talmudic chant) N.L. Saslavski (n.d.)

TEXT:
- IPA Transliteration
- **Sung Text**
- Word-for-Word Translation

IDIOMATIC TRANSLATION

aɪ aɪ aɪ aɪ aɪ aɪ
Ay ay ay ay ay ay…(etc.)
Ay ay ay ay ay ay

Ay ay ay ay ay ay…

maɪ kɔ maʃ.ma lɔn dɛɾ ɾɛ.gn̩
May - ko mashma lon der regn?
What is the meaning of the rain

vɔs ʒɜ lɔzt ʔɛɾ mɪr tsu hɛ.ɾn̩
Vos zhe lozt er mir tsu hern?
What then allows it me to hear

zaɪ.nɜ tɾɔ.pn̩s ʔɔif di ʃɔɪ.bn̩
Zayne tropns oyf di shoybn
Its drops on the window pane

kaɪk.lɜn zɪx   vi tɾi.bɜ tɾɛ.ɾn̩
Kayklen zikh   vi tribe trern.
Roll   themselves like gloomy tears

ʊn di ʃti.vl̩ ʔɪz tzɛ.'ɾɪ.sn̩
Un di shtivl iz tzerisn,
And the boot is torn

ʊn ɛs vɛɾt   ʔɪn gas ʔa blɔ.tɜ
Un es vert   in gas a blote;
And it becomes in road a mud

bald vɛt ʔɔix dɛɾ vɪn.tɜɾ kʊ.mɜn
Bald vet oykh der vinter kumen —
Soon will also the winter come

xhɔb kɛɪn 'va.ɾɜ.mɜ ka.'pɔ.tɜ
Kh'hob keyn vareme kapote...
I have no warm coat

What is the meaning of the rain?
What is it trying to teach me?
Its drops roll like gloomy tears
Down the windowpane.
My boot is torn,
And the street is getting muddy;
Soon, too, the winter will come,
And I have no warm coat…

maɪ kɔ maʃ.ma lɔn dɔs lɪx.tl̩
May - ko mashma lon dos likhtl?
What is the meaning of the candle

vɔs ʒɜ lɔzt ʔɛs mɪr tsu hɛ.ɾn̩
Vos zhe lozt es mir tsu hern?
What then allows it me to hear

ska.pɔt ʔʊn ɛs tɾɪft ʔɪr xɛɪ.lɜv
S'kapet un es trift ir kheylev
It drips and it drips its tallow

ʊns vɛt bald fʊn ʔɪr nɪt   vɛ.ɾn̩
Un's vet bald fun ir nit   vern.
And it will soon of it nothing become

a.'zɔɪ tsaŋk ʔɪx dɔ ʔɪn klaɪ.zl̩
Azoy tsank ikh do in klayzl,
Thus flicker I here in synagogue

What is the meaning of the candle?
What is it trying to teach me?
Its tallow drips and drips,
And soon there will be nothing left of it.
So do I, in this synagogue study room,

vi ʔa lɪx.tl̩ ʃvax ʔʊn tʊŋ.kl̩
Vi a likhtl, shvakh un tunkl,
Like a candle weak and dim

Flicker like a candle, weak and dim.

bɪz ʔɪx vɛl ʔa.ˈzɔɪ mɪɾ ʔɔɪs.gɛɪn
Biz ikh vel azoy mir oysgeyn
Until I will thus me go out

ɪn dɛɾ ʃtɪl ʔɪn mɪz.ɾɔx vɪŋ.kl̩
In der shtil, in mizrokh-vinkl...
In the silence in eastern corner

aɪ aɪ aɪ aɪ aɪ aɪ
Ay ay ay ay ay ay...(etc.)
Ay ay ay ay ay ay

Till finally I go out, in silence,
At the corner of the eastern wall…
Ay ay ay ay ay ay…

maɪ kɔ maʃ.ma lɔn dɛɾ zɛɪ.gɜɾ
May - ko mashma lon der zeyger?
What is the meaning of the clock

vɔs ʒɜ lɔzt ʔɛɾ mɪɾ tsu hɛ.ɾn̩
Vos zhe lozt er mir tsu hern?
What thus allows it me to hear

mɪt zaɪn gɛl.bn̩ ˈtsɪ.fɜɾ.ˈblɛ.tl̩
Mit zayn gelbn tsifer - bletl,
With its yellow dial

mɪt zaɪn klɪŋ.gɜn mɪt zaɪn ʃvɛ.ɾn̩
Mit zayn klingen, mit zayn shvern.
With its ringing with its swearing

sɪzan ˈʔɔn.gɜ.ʃtɛl.tɜ kɛɪ.lɜ
S'iz an ongeshtelte keyle,
It is a mechanical gadget

shɔt kɛɪn lɛ.bn̩ kɛɪn gɜ.ˈfi.ln̩
S'hot keyn lebn, keyn gefiln;
It has no life no feeling

kʊmt di ʃɔ dɔ mʊz ʔɛɾ ʃlɔ.gn̩
Kumt di sho, do muz er shlogn,
Comes the hour then must it strike

ɔn zaɪn ɾɔ.tsn̩ ʔɔn zaɪn vɪ.ln̩
On zayn rotsn, on zayn viln.
Without its choice without its will

What is the meaning of the clock?
What is it trying to teach me?
With its yellow dial,
With its ringing, with its swearing?
It's a mechanical gadget,
Without life, without feelings;
When the hour comes, it must strike,
Involuntarily and with no will.

maɪ kɔ maʃ.ma lɔn maɪn lɛ.bn̩
May - ko mashma lon mayn lebn?
What is the meaning of my life

vɔs ʒɜ lɔzt ʔɛs mɪɾ tsu hɛ.ɾn̩
Vos zhe lozt es mir tsu hern?
What thus allows it me to hear

fɔɪ.ln̩ vɛl.kn̩ ʔɪn dɛɾ ju.gn̩t
Foyln, velkn in der yugnt,
Decaying withering in the youth

faɾ dɛɾ tsaɪt faɾ.ˈɛl.tɜɾt vɛ.ɾn̩
Far der tsayt fareltert vern.
Before the time aged becoming

ɛsn̩ tɛg ʔʊn ʃlɪŋ.gɜn tɾɛ.ɾn̩
Esn teg un shlingen trern,
'Eating days' and drinking tears

ʃlɔ.fn̩ ʔa.fn̩ fɔɪst dɛm haɾ.tn̩
Shlofn afn foyst dem hartn;
Sleeping on a fist the hard one

tɛɪ.tn̩ dɔ di ʔɔɪ.lɜm ha.ze
Teytn do di oylem - haze
Dying here the world this

ʊn ʔɔɪf ʔɔɪ.lɜm ha.be vaɾ.tn̩
Un oyf oylem habe vartn...
And on world after waiting

What is the meaning of my life?
What is it trying to say to me?
Decaying, withering in my youth,
Growing old before my time,
Meals at others' homes,
Washed down with tears,
Sleeping upon my hard fist,
Killing the pleasures of this world
While waiting for the next.

7
May-ko mashma lon

Words by Abraham Reisen (1875-1953)
Music based on a Talmudic chant; arr. by N. Saslowsky (n.d.)

Arrangement by Robert De Cormier
(piano reduction by John Yaffé)

Freely, pensively (♩ = ca. 50)   *molto ritenuto*   *a tempo*

Ay ay ay ay ay ay... ay ay ay ay ay ay ay...

A tempo, ma calmo (♩ = 56-58)

ay ay ay... May-ko mash - ma lon der re - gn? Vos zhe lozt er mir tsu
(2.) mash - ma lon der zey - ger? Vos zhe lozt er mir tsu

he - rn? Zay - ne tro - pns oyf di shoy - bn kayk-len zikh vi tri - be
he - rn? Mit zayn gel - bn tsi-fer - ble - tl, mit zayn klin - gen, mit zayn

rit.   *a tempo*   *rit.*   *a tempo*

col canto

8
rit.
a tempo
tre - rn. Un di shti - vl iz tse - ri - sn, un es vert in gas a
shve - rn? S'iz an on - ge - shel - te key - le, s'hot keyn le - bn, keyn ge -
rit.
a tempo
12
rit.
a tempo
rall.
blo - te; Bald vet oykh der vin - ter ku - men — Kh'hob keyn va - re - me ka -
fi - ln, kumt di sho, dan muz er shlo - gn, on zayn rot - sn, on zayn
rit.
a tempo
rall.
B
Più mosso (♩= 106-120)
16
più appassionato
po - te… May - ko mash - ma lon dos likh - tl? Vos zhe lozt es mir tsu
vi - ln… May - ko mash - ma lon mayn le - bn? Vos zhe lozt es mir tsu
Più mosso (♩= 106-120)
mf

20

he - rn? S'ka - pet un es trift ir khey - lev un s'vet bald fun ir nit
he - rn? Foy - ln, vel - kn in der yu - gnt, far der tsayt far - el - tert

24   **Largamente** ($\quad$ = ca. 76-84)   *calando*

ve - rn. A - zoy tsank ikh do in klay - zl, vi a likh - tl, shvakh un
ve - rn. E - sn teg un shlin - gen tre - rn, Shlo - fn oyf dem bank, dem

Largamente ($\quad$ = ca. 76-84)   *calando*

28   **Tempo I, calmo**   *rit.*   *a tempo*   *rall.*

tun - kl, biz ikh vel a - zoy mir oys - geyn in der shtil, in miz - rokh -
har - tn, tey - tn do di oy - lem ha - ze— Un oyf oy - lem ha - be

Tempo I, calmo   *rit.*   *a tempo*   *rall.*

p

May-ko mashma lon

C
Freely, pensively (♩= ca. 50)
32
1. come sopra
vin - kl…
var - tn…
Ay ay ay ay ay ay…
ay ay ay ay ay ay ay…
Freely, pensively (♩= ca. 50)
come sopra
ped.
36
a tempo
freely
a tempo
molto ritenuto
ay ay ay ay ay ay…
2. May ko -
a tempo
a tempo
molto ritenuto
col canto
p espr.
39
2. come sopra
Ay ay ay ay ay ay…
ay ay ay ay ay ay ay…
molto ritenuto
col canto
ten.

'Lost years are worse than lost money'
('Farlorene yorn iz erger vi farlorene gelt')

– Yiddish proverb

8
Oy, dortn, dortn
ibern vaserl

This song reflects the bittersweet circumstances of so many Jewish families from Eastern Europe in the nineteenth and twentieth centuries, kept apart by the need to seek work in a far-off country. It is a musical love letter from a young man (possibly gone off to the New World to put down new roots) to his sweetheart 'back home'. Not just emigration, but also the brutality of the military recruiting policy of the old Russian Empire led to many separations of sweethearts and family members. 'Oy, dortn, dortn ibern vaserl' expresses a young man's heartbreak over the delays and distance that keep him from fulfilling his dream of union with his beloved.

After World War II, folklorist Ruth Rubin began collecting old Yiddish folk songs from immigrants to North America. In her findings, she points out that, although it is intensely Jewish in its language and theme, 'Oy, dortn' is structurally very similar to certain older, mainstream German folk songs. This is typical of the mixed heritage of the Yiddish folk repertoire.

N.B. Regarding the 'rozeve papir' mentioned in the song: Apparently, pink crepe paper, dampened and applied to the lips, served nicely as a form of lipstick for young romantic girls in the Eastern European *shetl* (small rural villages) of the nineteenth century.

8
Oy, dortn, dortn ibern vaserl

ɔɪ	dɔɾ.tn̩	dɔɾ.tn̩	ʔi.bɜɾn̩	va.sɜɾl̩
Oy	**dortn,**	**dortn**	**ibern**	**vaserl**
Oh	there,	there	across the	water

(Anonymous)

TEXT:
- IPA Transliteration
- **Sung Text**
- Word-for-Word Translation

IDIOMATIC TRANSLATION

dɔɾ.tn̩	dɔɾ.tn̩	ʔi.bɜɾn̩	va.sɜɾl̩
Dortn,	**dortn,**	**ibern**	**vaserl;**
There	there	across the	water

ɔɪ	dɔɾ.tn̩	dɔɾ.tn̩	ʔi.bɜɾn̩	bɾɪk
Oy	**dortn,**	**dortn,**	**ibern**	**brik!**
Oh	there	there	across the	bridge

faɾ.'tri.bn̩	hɔt	mɛn	mɪx	ʔɪn	di	'vaɪ.tɜ.nɜ	lɛn.dɜɾ
Fartribn	**hot**	**men**	**mikh**	**in**	**di**	**vaytene**	**lender;**
Driven	has	one	me	in	the	distant	lands

ʊn	bɛn.kɜn	bɛnk	ʔɪx	nɔx	dɪɾ	tsu.'ɾɪk
Un	**benken**	**benk**	**ikh**	**nokh**	**dir**	**tsurik**
And	yearning	yearn	I	for	you	return

There across the water,
Oh, there across the bridge!
I have been driven into distant lands,
And I yearn to be with you again!

ɔɪ	hɛlf	mɪɾ	'gɔ.tɜn.ju	ʔɔɪ	gɔt	ʔɪn	hɪ.ml̩
Oy,	**helf**	**mir,**	**Gotenyu,**	**oy,**	**Got**	**in**	**himl;**
Oh	help	me	dear God	oh	God	in	heaven

ɔɪ	hɛlf	mɪɾ	'gɔ.tɜ.nju	sɪz	mɪɾ	nɪt	gʊt
Oy,	**helf**	**mir,**	**Gotenyu,**	**s'iz**	**mir**	**nit**	**gut!**
Oh	help	me	dear God	it is	me	not	good

ʃɔɪn	tsaɪt	dɾaɪ	'jɔ.ɾɜ.lɜx	vi	mɪɾ	ʃpiln̩	ʔa	li.bɜ
Shoyn	**tsayt**	**dray**	**yorelekh,**	**vi**	**mir**	**shpiln**	**a**	**libe;**
Already	since	three	years	how	we	act	a	love

ʊn	ʃpiln̩	di	li.bɜ	kɛ.nɜn	mɪɾ	nɪt
Un	**shpiln**	**di**	**libe**	**kenen**	**mir**	**nit!**
And	act	the	love	can	we	not

Oh, help me, dear God, oh God in heaven;
Oh, help me, dear God, I feel so blue!
For three years, we've been courting,
And we still cannot fulfill our love.

ɔɪ	daɪ.nɜ	'ʔɔɪ.gɜ.lɜx	vi	di	ʃvaɾ.tsɜ	'kɛɾ.ʃɜ.lɜx
Oy,	**dayne**	**oygelekh,**	**vi**	**di**	**shvartse**	**kershelekh,**
Oh	your	eyes	like	the	black	cherries

ʊn	daɪ.nɜ	'lɪ.pɜ.lɜx	vi	'ɾɔ.zɜ.vɜ	pa.pɪɾ
Un	**dayne**	**lipelekh,**	**vi**	**rozeve**	**papir.**
And	your	lips	like	pink	paper

ʊn	daɪ.nɜ	'fɪŋ.gɜɾ.lɜx	vi	tɪnt	ʔʊn	vi	fɛ.dɜɾ
Un	**dayne**	**fingerlekh,**	**vi**	**tint**	**un**	**vi**	**feder**
And	your	fingers	like	ink	and	like	pen

ɔɪ	ʃɾaɪ.bn̩	zɔl.stu	ʔɔf.tɜ	bɾɪv	tsu	mɪɾ
Oy,	**shraybn**	**zolstu**	**ofte**	**briv**	**tsu**	**mir!**
Oh	write	should you	often	letters	to	me

Oh, your eyes, like little black cherries,
Your lips, like pink paper;
And your little fingers, like pen and ink:
Oh, do write me letters often!

8
Oy, dortn, dortn ibern vaserl

(Anonymous)

Arrangement by Robert De Cormier
(piano reduction by John Yaffé)

14 poco rit. a tempo B

ikh nokh dir tsu - rik!_____ Oy, helf mir, go-ten - yu, oy, got in hi -

20

ml; Oy, helf mir, go - ten yu, s'iz__ mir nit gut!_____ Shoyn

25

tsayt dray yo - re - lekh, vi mir shpi - ln a li - be; Un shpiln di li - be

30 poco rit. a tempo C

ke - nen mir nit!_____ Oy, day - ne oy - ge -

legato

Oy dortn, dortn ibern vaserl

'Yiddish wasn't just words, you see, it was attitude. It was sweet and sour. It was a shrug and a kiss. It was humility and defiance all in one'.

— **Erica Jong**, American novelist, satirist, and poet

9
Reb Motenyu
(or "Bom-bom,
biri-biri-bom)

As with the songs 'A nign', 'Dona dona dona', and 'Tum-balalayke' in this anthology, this song is a form of *ballad*, in which the singer assumes the role of storyteller; and as with the song 'A dudele', it is exemplary of the very personal relationship the Jewish people have with God. Like the character Tevye in the musical *Fiddler on the Roof*, it is not uncommon for Jews to converse directly with God, and not only during prayer.

In this case, the persona of the song is a rebe (*rabbi*). He engages with God in a prayer at the close of an arduous day.

According to Leybl Botwinik:

> 'The day is long, the war is difficult' are a few words from this well-known song. When the tribes of Israel were about to enter the land of Israel after forty years of wandering in the desert, there were several tribes that wanted to remain on the other side of the Jordan River, and not enter the holy land. They had their reasons. However, when it came to the 'moment of truth' — to wage war to conquer Canaan and remake it into the Land of Israel — they overcame their personal desires and did not shirk their duty or apathetically stand aside to let others do the work. Instead, they stood firm and united with their brothers and worked together for the common cause.

In this song, the rebe asks God to be merciful, to acknowledge him for the virtue of his actions, and to thus grant him a peaceful night's sleep. The song touches on matters of duty, punishment, grace, forgiveness, the necessity of war, and righteousness and evil. It is a very personal and ardent expression of faith and reverence for 'The Eternal'.

9

**Reb Motenyu
(or "Bom-bom,
biri-biri-bom)**

ɾɛb 'mɔ.tɜ.nju (zɛmɜɾ)
Reb Motenyu (or Zemer, or Bim-bom, biri-biri-bom)
Rabbi Motenyu (Tune)

Words: Aaron Zeitlin (1889-1973)
Music: Samuel Bugatch (1898-1984)

TEXT:
- IPA Transliteration
- **Sung Text**
- Word-for-Word Translation

| **IDIOMATIC TRANSLATION** |

Mmm...

Mmm...

bɔm bɔm bi.ɾi bi.ɾi bɔm
Bom bom biri - biri - bom...(etc.)
Bom bom biri biri bom

Bom-bom, biri-biri-bom...(etc.)

zɔgt dɛɾ ɾɛ.bɛ ɾɛb 'mɔ.tɜ.nju
Zogt der rebe reb Motenyu:
Says the rabbi Rabbi Motenyu

a gʊt mɔr.gn̩ dɪɾ 'gɔ.tɜ.nju
A gut morgn dir Gotenyu!
A good morning to you dear God

nɛm ʔa.'ɾɔp fʊn ʔʊndz daɪn kas
Nem arop fun undz dayn kas,
Take down from us your wrath

vɛt mɛn tɔn kɛ.'dɪn 've.kɜ.das
Vet men ton kedin vekedas.
Will one to do according to your law

Rabbi Motenyu says,
"Good morning to you, dear God!
Remove your wrath from us,
And we'll act according to your laws."

ɔɪ tsa.'di.kɪm tsa.'di.kɪm gɛɪ.ɜn bɔm
Oy tsadikim tsadikim geyen bom;
Oh the righteous the righteous go bom

ɔɪ ɾɜ.'ʃɔ.jɪm ɾɜ.'ʃɔ.jɪm fa.ln̩ bɔm
Oy reshoyim reshoyim faln bom.
Oh the wicked the wicked fall bom

bɔm bɔm bi.ɾi bi.ɾi bɔm
Bom bom biri - biri - bom...(etc.)
Bom bom biri biri bom

Oh, the righteous rise up;
Oh, the wicked fall down.
Bom-bom, biri-biri-bom...

zɔgt dɛɾ ɾɛ.bɛ ɾɛb 'mɔ.tɜ.nju
Zogt der rebe reb Motenyu:
Says the rabbi Rabbi Motenyu

a gʊt hɛlf dɪɾ 'gɔ.tɜ.nju
A gut helf dir Gotenyu!
A good afternoon to you dear God

dɛɾ tɔg ʔɪz hɛɪs di mɪl.'xɔ.mɜ ʔɪz ʃvɛɾ
Der tog iz heys di milkhome iz shver;
The day is hot the war is difficult

nɔɾ mɛn lɔzt nɪt ʔa.'ɾɔɪs dɔs gɜ.'vɛɾ
Nor men lozt nit aroys dos gever.
Only one releases not forth the weapons

Rabbi Motenyu says,
"Good afternoon to you, dear God!
The day is hot, and the war is bitter;
But no one will lay down his weapons."

ɔɪ tsa.'di.kɪm
Oy tsadikim...(etc.)
Oh the righteous

Oh, the righteous rise up...(etc.)

zɔgt dɛɾ ɾɛ.bɛ ɾɛb 'mɔ.tɜ.nju
Zogt der rebe reb Motenyu:
Says the rabbi Rabbi Motenyu

a gʊt nɔ.vn̩t dɪɾ 'gɔ.tɜ.nju
A gut n'ovnt dir Gotenyu!
A good evening to you dear God

dɛɾ tɔg ʔɪz a.vɛk ʔɪx hɔb ʔalts gɜ.'maxt
Der tog iz avek ikh hob alts gemakht;
The day is gone I have everything done

gɪb ʒɜ mɪɾ ʔa 'gʊ.tɪŋ.kɜ naxt
Gib zhe mir a gutinke nakht
Give then to me a good night

Rabbi Motenyu says,
"Good evening to you, dear God!
The day is over, I've done what I had to;
Grant me a peaceful night."

ɔɪ tsa.'di.kɪm
Oy tsadikim…(etc.)
Oh the righteous

Oh, the righteous rise up…(etc.)

9
Reb Motenyu
(or 'Bom-bom, biri-biri-bom')

Words by Aaron Zeitlin (1889-1973)
Music by Samuel Bugatch (1898-1984)

Arrangement by Robert De Cormier
(piano reduction by John Yaffé)

Reb Motenyu

70

B **More flowing, freely**
colla voce

25

1. Zogt der re - be, reb Mo - te - nyu: A gut - mor - gn dir, Go - te - nyu!
2. Zogt der re - be, reb Mo - te - nyu: A gut - helf___ undz, Go - te - nyu! Der
3. Zogt der re - be, reb Mo - te - nyu: A gut - o - vnt dir, Go - te - nyu! Der

More flowing, freely
colla voce

29 *a tempo*

Nem a - rop fun undz dayn___ kas,___ vet men ton___ ke -
tog iz heys, di mil - kho - me iz shver;___ Nor men lozt___ nit a -
tog iz a - vek, ikh hob alts ge - makht;___ Gib zhe mir___ a

a tempo

32 *rit.*   *a tempo*

din___ ve - ke - das.   Nem a - rop fun undz dayn___ kas,___
roys___ dos ge - ver. Der tog iz heys, di mil - kho - me iz shver;___
gu - tin - ke nakht. Der tog iz a - vek, ikh hob alts ge - makht;___

a tempo

rit.

Reb Motenyu

35
rit.
C holding back
vet men ton ke - din ve - ke - das. Oy, tsa -
Nor men lozt nit a - roys dos ge - ver. Oy, tsa -
Gib zhe mir a gu - tin - ke nakht. Oy, tsa -
holding back
rit.
f
38
more flowing
holding back
di - kim, tsa - di - kim gey - en bom; Oy re -
di - kim, tsa - di - kim gey - en bom; Oy re -
di - kim, tsa - di - kim gey - en bom; Oy re -
more flowing
holding back
mf
f
D Moderato (𝅗𝅥 = 66-70)
42
a tempo
rit.
1./2.
sho - yim, re - sho - yim fa - (ln) bom. Bom - - bom,
sho - yim, re - sho - yim fa - - (ln) bom. Bom - - bom,
sho - yim, re - sho - yim fa - - (ln) bom.
a tempo
rit.
Moderato (𝅗𝅥 = 66-70)
mf
(p)

46

bi - ri - bi - ri - bom,_____ bim - bom, bim - bom, bi - ri - bi - ri - bom;
bi - ri - bi - ri - bom,_____ bim - bom, bim - bom, bi - ri - bi - ri - bom - bom - bom - bom;

49   *poco accel.*   *rall. molto*

Bom - bom,   bi - ri - bi - ri - bom,_____ bim - bom, bi - ri - bi - ri - bom.
Bom - bom,   bi - ri - bi - ri - bom,_____ bim - bom, bi - ri - bi - ri - bom.

poco accel.

(p)

rall. molto

E **Moderato** (♩= 66-70)

53 [3.

Bom - bom,   bi - ri - bi - ri - bom,_____ bim - bom, bim - bom,   bi - ri - bi - ri - bom - bom - bom - bom;

Moderato (♩= 66-70)

p ma marc.

Reb Motenyu

57
Bom - - bom, bi - ri - bi - ri - bom, bim - bom, bi - ri - bi - ri -
60
poco accel.
Poco più mosso
bom. Bom - - bom, bi - ri - bi - ri - bom,
poco accel.
Poco più mosso
(p)
63
bim - bom, bim - bom, bi - ri - bi - ri - bom - bom - bom - bom; Bom - bom,
(p)
66
rall. molto
bi - ri - bi - ri - bom, bim - bom, bi - ri - bi - ri - bom.
rall. molto
pp
ped.

'The sea has no shore — Learning has no end'
('Der yam on a breg — Di toyre on an ek')

– Yiddish proverb

10
Rozhinkes mit mandlen

This beloved song is probably the most famous of the songs written by Abraham Goldfaden, founder of the modern Yiddish theatre. In fact, however, it is a traditional Jewish lullaby *popularized in the arrangement by Goldfaden*, done for his 1880 Yiddish musical play *Shulamis*.* 'Rozhinkes' is a lullaby to which countless children have been sung to sleep since Goldfaden brought it out, and it has become so well known that it has assumed the status of a classic folk song.

Many feel that the name 'Yidele' is a metaphor for the Jewish people as a whole. The Jewish people were always having to pack up, move, and start up their lives again to assure their survival. One of the ways to make a living was to peddle goods as itinerant salesmen. So, in this song, the widow tells the baby to sleep now and rest, for his life will be full of traveling — selling raisins and almonds.

The *klor vays tsigele* (small white goat) mentioned in the song is a familiar figure in Jewish folklore, art, and literature, from 'Chad Gadya' — the Aramaic song Jews sing each year at the Passover *seder* — through to the present day. Goats float through Marc Chagall's paintings, they snore through Yiddish lullabies, and they appear in poems and stories by many Yiddish writers. Jews celebrated goats because they lived with goats: even the poorest *shtetl* (Eastern European rural village) family kept a goat tethered in front of the house to provide milk for the children. However, the image is less fanciful than it appears: on cold winter nights, Jews often invited their innocent creature to sleep inside the house. Jews identified with their small, humble, but intelligent animal, so much so that the *tsigele* became a symbol of the Jewish people — and, by the way, of the Yiddish Book Center in Amherst, Massachusetts.

'Rozhinkes mit mandlen' can be found in multiple translations and multiple versions, with slight variations in both the Yiddish and English lyrics. It has been recorded as both a vocal and instrumental work by many famous artists over the years, including violinist Itzhak Perlman, folk singer Chava Alberstein and opera singer Benita Valente. One verse of the song appears even in the Herman Wouk novel *War and Remembrance* — in Yiddish as well as an English translation — and also in the television mini-series based on the same book.

* The provenance of the refrain is an older Yiddish folk lullaby, 'Unter Yankeles ['dem kind's'?] vigele'.

	'rɔ.ʒɪŋ.kɜs mɪt mand.lɜn
10	**Rozhinkes mit mandlen**
Rozhinkes mit	Raisins with Almonds
mandlen	Words: Partially attr. to Abraham Goldfaden (1840-1908)
	Music: Anonymous

TEXT:
- IPA Transliteration
- **Sung Text**
- Word-for-Word Translation

IDIOMATIC TRANSLATION

ɪn dɛm 'bɛɪs-ha.'mɪk.dɔʃ
In dem beys-hamikdosh,
In The Temple

ɪn a vɪŋ.kl̩ xɛɪ.dɜr
in a vinkl kheyder
in a corner Torah study room

zɪtst di ʔal.'mɔ.nɜ
zitst di almone
Sits the widow

bas.'tsi.ɔn ʔa.'lɛɪn
bas-tsion aleyn;
Bas-Tsion alone

ɪr bɛn 'jɔ.xɪ.dl̩ 'ji.dɛ.lɜn
Ir ben-yokhidl yidelen
Her son Yidele

vɪgt zi kɛ.'sɛɪ.dɜr
vigt zi keseyder,
rocks she endlessly

ʊn zɪŋt ʔim tsʊm ʃlɔ.fn̩
Un zingt im tsum shlofn
And sings him to sleep

a 'li.dɛ.lɜ ʃɛɪn
a lidele sheyn.
a (little)song lovely

aɪ lu lu lu
Ay lu lu lu…
Ay lu lu lu

In The Temple,
In the corner of a room,
Sits Bas-Tsion the widow, alone;
Endlessly rocking her son Yidele
And sings him to sleep with a sweet lullaby.
Ay lu lu lu…

ʊn.tɜr 'ji.dɛ.lɜz 'vi.gɛ.lɜ
Unter yideles vigele
Under Yidele's cradle

ʃtɛɪt a klɔr vaɪs 'tsi.gɛ.lɜ
shteyt a klor vays tsigele.
Stands a clear white goat

dɔs 'tsi.gɛ.lɜ ʔɪz gɜ.'fɔ.rn̩ hand.lɜn
Dos tsigele iz geforn handlen.
The goat has gone to market

dɔs vɛt zaɪn daɪn ba.'ruf
Dos vet zayn dayn baruf:
This will be your calling

'rɔ.ʒɪŋ.kɜs mɪt mand.lɜn
Rozhinkes mit mandlen.
Raisins with almonds

ʃlɔf ʒɜ 'ji.dɛ.lɜ ʃlɔf
Shlof zhe yidele Shlof.
Sleep you Yidele Sleep

aɪ lu lu lu
Ay lu lu lu…
Ay lu lu lu

Under Yidele's cradle
Stands a snow-white little goat.
The goat has travelled to sell his wares.
That will be your calling, too,
Trading in raisins and almonds.
Sleep now, Yidele, sleep.
Ay lu lu lu…

10
Rozhinkes mit mandlen

Words and Music attributed partially to
Abraham Goldfaden (1840-1908)

Arrangement by Robert De Cormier
(piano reduction by John Yaffé)

In dem beys ha-mik-dosh, in a vin-kl
khey-der, zitst di al-mo-ne bas tsi-on a-leyn; Ir ben yo-chi-dl
yi-de-len vigt si ke-sey-der, un zingt im tsum shlo-fn a li-de-le

16
(plaintively)
sheyn... ay lu lu lu. Un-ter
ped.
21
B
a tempo
yi - de - les vi - - - ge - le shteyt a klor vays
a tempo
p
26
tsi - - ge - le. Dos tsi-ge-le iz ge-fo - - rn

31
hand - len;
Dos vet zayn dayn ba - ruf:
espr.
36
Ro - - zhin - kes mit mand - len…
espr.
41
rallentando
Shlof - zhe yi - de - le, shlof…
ay lu lu lu.
rallentando
f espr.
ped.

Dos tsi-ge-le iz ge-fo - - rn hand-len;___

Dos vet zayn dayn ba - ruf...___

Ro - -zhin-kes___ mit mand-len...___ Shlof - zhe

yi - de - le, shlof..._____ Mm..._____

E

Mm..._____ Shlof - zhe

ritenuto

col canto

ritenuto

yi - de - le, shlof..._____ ay__ lu__ lu__ lu._____

a tempo

(*calmo*)

a tempo

ped._____

Rozhinkes mit mandlen

'A person is sometimes stronger than iron and sometimes weaker than a fly'
('A mentsh iz a mol shtarker fun ayzn un a mol shvakher fun a flig')

– Yiddish proverb

11
S'brent

Following a *pogrom** in the Polish town Przytyk in 1936, Mordecai Gebirtig wrote this stirring song, which was to prove prophetic of the Holocaust.** Gebirtig appeals to his brothers and sisters not to stand passively and watch helplessly as their village burns, but to seize what they can and put down the fire, even with their own blood. During World War II, 'S'brent' became popular in the Kraków (Poland) ghetto*** and inspired young people to take up arms against the Nazis. It spread to many other ghettos and concentration camps and was translated into Polish as well as several other languages. It became an anthem of the Jewish resistance.

Gebirtig, born in 1877 in Kraków, Poland, was a Yiddish folk poet and songwriter. He was killed in June 1942 during a roundup of Jews for deportation from the Kraków ghetto to concentration camps. Since then, the song, in the original Yiddish and in its Hebrew translation titled 'Ha-Ayyarah Bo'eret' ('Our Little Town is Burning!') — hence the occasional reference to a Yiddish title 'Undzer shtetl brent!' — continues to be widely performed in the context of Holocaust commemorations.

pogrom: A form of violent attack, condoned by the government or military authorities, and directed toward a particular ethnic or religious group. In these attacks, people are killed, tortured, and/or raped, and their homes, businesses, properties, and religious centres destroyed.

**Holocaust*: A genocide during World War II, in which Nazi Germany, aided by local collaborators in various other countries, systematically murdered some six million European Jews — around two-thirds of the Jewish population of Europe — between 1941 and 1945.

***ghetto*: A part of a city in which members of a minority group live, typically as a result of social, legal, or economic pressure. During World War II, the regime of Nazi Germany set up ghettos across occupied Europe in order to segregate and confine Jews, and sometimes Romani people, into small sections of towns and cities, furthering their exploitation.

11
S'brent

sbɾɛnt
S'brent!
It's Burning!

Words and music: Mordechai Gebirtig (1877-1942)

TEXT:
- IPA Transliteration
- **Sung Text**
- Word-for-Word Translation

| | **IDIOMATIC TRANSLATION** |

---

sbɾɛnt   'bɾi.dɛr.lɔx   sbɾɛnt
S'brent!   Briderlekh, s'brent!
It's burning brothers   it's burning

ɔɪ ʔʊnd.zɛɾ ʔɔ.ɾɛm ʃtɛ.tl̩ nɛ.bɔx bɾɛnt
Oy, undzer   orem   shtetl nebekh brent
Oh   our   poor   village badly   burns

bɛɪ.zɜ vɪn.tn̩ mɪt jɪɾ.'gɔ.zn̩
Beyze vintn mit yirgozn,
Angry winds with rage

ɾaɪ.sn̩ bɾɛ.xn̩ ʔʊn tsɛ.'blɔ.zn̩
Raysn, brekhn un tseblozn;
Tearing shattering and exploding

ʃtaɾ.kɜɾ nɔx di vɪl.dɜ fla.mɜn
Shtarker nokh di vilde flamen,
Stronger still the wild flames

alts ʔa.'ɾʊm ʃɔɪn bɾɛnt
Alts   arum shoyn brent!
Everything around already burns

ʊn ʔiɾ ʃtɛɪt ʔʊn kʊkt ʔa.'zɔɪ zɪx
Un ir shteyt un kukt azoy zikh,
And you stand and look thus yourself

mɪt faɾ.'lɛɪg.tɜ hɛnt
Mit farleygte hent,
With folded hands

ʊn ʔiɾ ʃtɛɪt ʔʊn kʊkt ʔa.'zɔɪ zɪx
Un ir shteyt un kukt azoy zikh;
And you stand and look thus yourself

ʊnd.zɜɾ ʃtɛ.tl̩ bɾɛnt
Undzer shtetl brent!
Our village burns

It's burning, brothers, it's burning!
Oh, our poor village is burning horribly!
Angry winds rage,
Tearing, shattering, and exploding;
The wild flames are becoming stronger,
And everything is on fire!
And you stand there, looking on,
With your hands folded,
You stand there, looking on;
Our village is burning!

---

sbɾɛnt   'bɾi.dɜɾ.lɔx   sbɾɛnt
S'brent!   Briderlekh, s'brent!
It's burning brothers   it's burning

ɔɪ ʔʊnd.zɛɾ ʔɔ.ɾɛm ʃtɛ.tl̩ nɛ.bɔx bɾɛnt
Oy, undzer   orem   shtetl nebekh brent!
Oh, our   poor   village badly   burns

sɔ.bn̩ ʃɔɪn di 'faɪ.ɜɾ.tsʊŋ.gɜn
S'hobn shoyn di fayertsungen
It has already the tongues of fire

dɔs gan.tsɜ ʃtɛtl̩ 'aɪn.gɜ.ʃlʊŋ.gɜn
Dos gantse shtetl ayngeshlungen
The entire village swallowed

ʊn di bɛɪ.zɜ vɪn.tn̩ hu.ʒɜn
Un di beyze vintn huzhen;
And the angry winds howl

ʊnd.zɜɾ ʃtɛ.tl̩ bɾɛnt
Undzer shtetl brent!
Our village burns

It's burning, brothers, it's burning!
Oh, our poor village is burning horribly!
Tongues of fire have already
Swallowed up the entire village,
And the angry winds howl;
Our village burns!

ʊn ʔir ʃteɪt ʔʊn kʊkt ʔa.'zɔɪ zɪx
Un ir shteyt un kukt azoy zikh...(etc.)
And you stand and look thus yourself

> And you stand there, looking on...(etc.)

sbrɛnt 'bri.dɔr.lɔx sbrɛnt
S'brent! Briderlekh, s'brent!
It's burning brothers it's burning

ɔɪ ʔɛs kɛn xɔ.'li.lɔ kʊ.mɔn dɛr mɔ.'mɛnt
Oy, es ken kholile kumen der moment:
Oh it can God forbid come the moment

ʊnd.zɔr ʃtɔt mɪt ʔʊndz tsu.'za.mɔn
Undzer shtot mit undz tsuzamen
Our village with us together

zɔl ʔaf ʔaʃ ʔa.'vɛk ʔɪn fla.mɔn
Zol af ash avek in flamen,
Should into ash away in flames

blaɪ.bɔn zɔl vi nɔx ʔa ʃlaxt
Blayben zol — vi nokh a shlakht —
Remain will like after a slaughter

nɔr pʊs.tɔ ʃvar.tsɔ vɛnt
Nor puste, shvartse vent!
Only empty black walls

ʊn ʔir ʃteɪt ʔʊn kʊkt ʔa.'zɔɪ zɪx
Un ir shteyt un kukt azoy zikh...(etc.)
And you stand and look such yourself

> It's burning, brothers, it's burning!
> Oh, God forbid, at any moment
> Our village, and all of us in it,
> Could burn into a billow of ash;
> And all that would remain,
> As in the aftermath of a massacre,
> Would be idle black walls!
> And you stand there, looking on...(etc.)

sbrɛnt 'bri.dɔr.lɔx sbrɛnt
S'brent! Briderlekh, s'brent!
It's burning brothers it's burning

di hɪlf ʔɪz nɔr ʔɪn ʔaɪx ʔa.'lɛɪn gɔ.'vɛndt
Di hilf iz nor in aykh aleyn gevendt;
The help is only on you alone turned

ɔɪb dɔs ʃtɛ.tl̩ ʔɪz ʔaɪx taɪ.ɔr
Oyb dos shtetl iz aykh tayer,
If the village is to you dear

nɛmt di kɛɪ.lɔm lɛʃt dɔs faɪ.ɔr
Nemt di keylim, lesht dos fayer;
Take the buckets extinguish the fire

lɛʃt mɪt ʔaɪ.ɔr ʔɛɪ.gn̩ blʊt
Lesht mit ayer eygn blut —
Extinguish with your own blood

ba.'vaɪzt ʔaz ʔir dɔs kɛnt
Bavayzt, az ir dos kent
Prove that you this can

ʃtɛɪt nɪt bri.dɔr ʔɔt ʔa.'zɔɪ zɪx
Shteyt nit, brider, ot azoy zikh
Stand not brother there so yourself

mɪt far.'lɛɪg.tɔ hɛnt
Mit farleygte hent;
With folded hands

ʃtɛɪt nɪt bri.dɔr lɛʃt dɔs faɪ.ɔr
Shteyt nit, brider, lesht dos fayer —
Stand not brother extinguish the fire

ʊnd.zɔr ʃtɛ.tl̩ brɛnt
Undzer shtetl brent!
Our village is burning

> It's burning, brothers, it's burning!
> Help can come only from you;
> If your village is dear to you,
> Fetch some buckets and put out the fire;
> Extinguish it with your own blood —
> Prove that you can do it!
> Don't just stand there, looking on,
> With your hands folded;
> Don't just stand there, put out the fire.
> Our village is burning!

11
S'brent

Words and music by
Mordechai Gebirtig (1877-1942)

Arrangement by Robert De Cormier
(piano reduction by John Yaffé)

Freely and dramatically

a tempo

S'brent!____ Bri - der - lekh, s'brent!____

A

S'brent!____ Bri - der - lekh, s'brent!____ Oy, und - zer o - rem shte - tl ne - bekh

Tempo giusto (♩=ca. 86)

brent!____ Bey - ze vin - tn mit yir - go - zn, ray - sn, bre - khn un tse - blo - zn;

Shtar - ker nokh di vil - de fla - men, alts a - rum shoyn brent.

Un ir shteyt un kukt a - zoy zikh, mit far - leyg - te hent; Un ir shteyt un kukt a - zoy sikh —

Und - zer shte - tl brent!____ S'brent!____ Bri - der - lekh, s'brent!____ Oy,

und - zer o - rem shte - tl ne - bekh brent!____ S'ho - bn shoyn di fa - yer - tsun - gen

S'brent

22
dos gan - tse shte - tl ayn - ge - shlun - gen — Un di bey - ze vin - tn hu - zhen,
24
und - zer she - tl brent! Un ir shteyt un kukt a - zoy zikh,
f
sub. p
26
mit far - leyg - te hent; Un ir shteyt un kukt a - zoy sikh — Und - zer shte - tl brent!
gl.
29
C
a tempo
S'brent! Bri - der - lekh, s'brent! Oy, es
a tempo
3
f
p
pp
f

ken kho - li - le ku - men der mo - ment:____ Und - zer shtot mit undz tsu - za - men

zol af ash a - vek in fla - men, blay - ben zol, vi nokh a shlakht,_ nor pus - te, shvar - tse vent!

Un ir shteyt un kukt a - zoy zikh, mit far - leyg - te hent; Shteyt nit, bri - der, lesht dos fa - yer —

Und - zer shte - tl brent!____ S'brent!____ Bri - der - lekh, s'brent!____ Di

S'brent

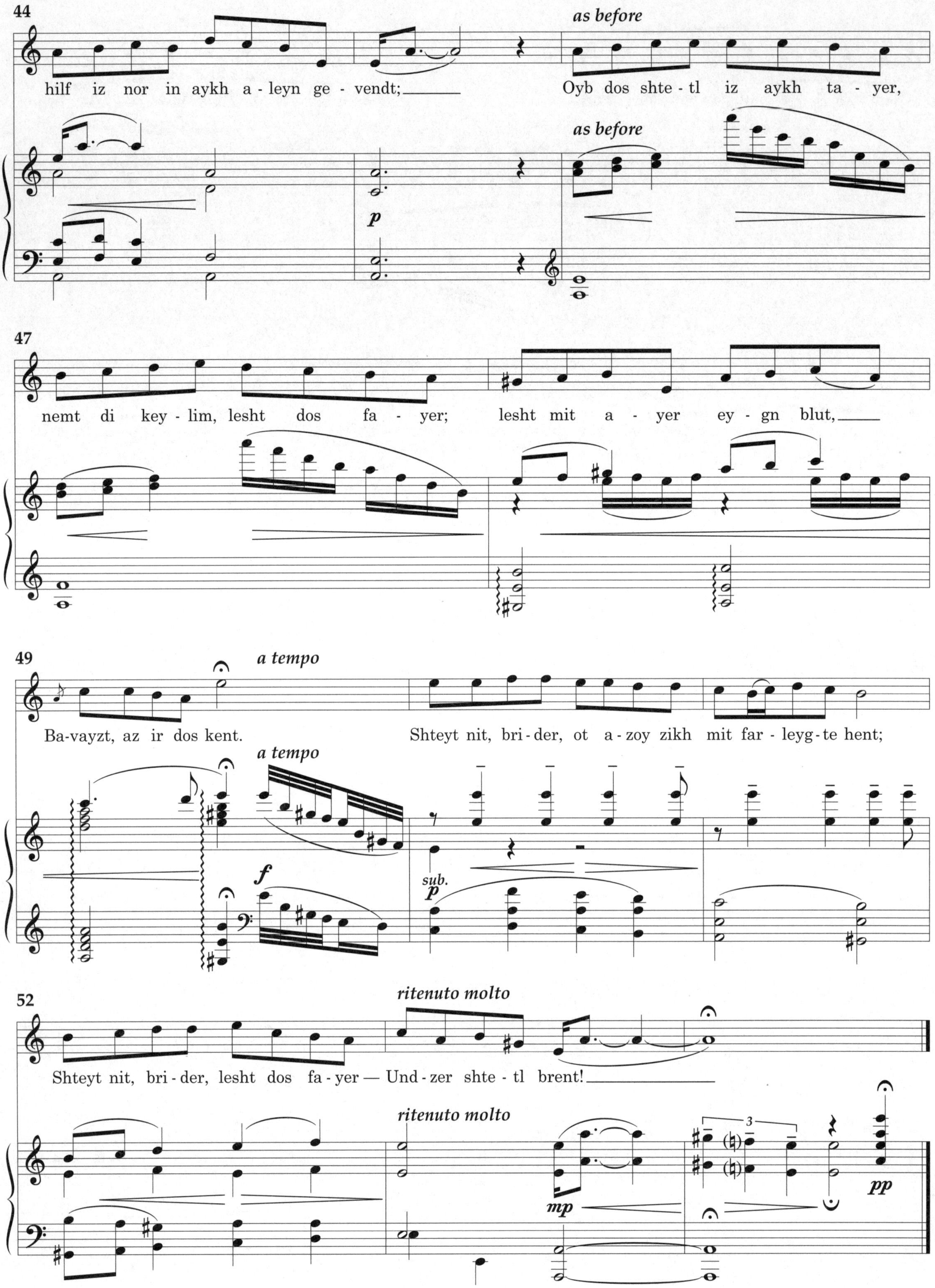
44
as before
hilf iz nor in aykh a - leyn ge - vendt;
Oyb dos shte - tl iz aykh ta - yer,
as before
p
47
nemt di key - lim, lesht dos fa - yer;
lesht mit a - yer ey - gn blut,
49
a tempo
Ba - vayzt, az ir dos kent.
Shteyt nit, bri - der, ot a - zoy zikh mit far - leyg - te hent;
a tempo
f
sub. p
52
ritenuto molto
Shteyt nit, bri - der, lesht dos fa - yer — Und - zer shte - tl brent!
ritenuto molto
3
mp
pp

12
S'dremlen feygl oyf di tsvaygn

This song was written by Leah Rudnicki while in the Jewish ghetto* at Vilnius (Lithuania). Rudnicki (born in Kalvarija, Lithuania) was a member of the editorial staff of the newspaper *Vilner emes* and a member of the resistance movement — a *partisan*.* She was caught by the Gestapo and deported to the concentration camp at Majdanek (Poland) in September 1943, where she died.

Folklorist Ruth Rubin recounts the history of 'S'dremlen feygl oyf di tsvaygn' in her *A Treasury of Jewish Folksong*. Apparently, Rudnicki heard of a three-year-old child found alive after a massacre of some 4,000 Jews by the Nazis in Ponar (Lithuania). She wrote this lullaby for the child, left fatherless and motherless, the words set to an earlier Yiddish song melody 'S'iz keyn broyt in shtub nishto' (words by Izi Charik, music by Leyb Yampolski). The song came to be known as the 'Lullaby of the Ghetto', the Jewish ghetto established and operated by the Nazis in the city of Vilnius during World War II.

The absence of a father is a theme frequently mentioned in lullabies: fathers left their families to forge a new life in the New World (e.g., 'Shlof, mayn kind' [Sleep, My Child], by Sholem Aleichem); and even when the families were reunited, fathers seldom had time to spend with their children (e.g., 'Mayn yingele' [My Little Boy]). Lullabies sung during the Holocaust sometimes expressed the horrors of orphanhood. In this song, Rudnicki describes a child who has lost everything, even his father and mother. A stranger sings by the baby's cradle. Singer Marthe Schlamme wrote that she rarely performed this song because it affected her too deeply, and she found it difficult to control her voice while singing it.

ghetto: A part of a city in which members of a minority group live, typically as a result of social, legal, or economic pressure. During World War II, the regime of Nazi Germany set up ghettos across occupied Europe in order to segregate and confine Jews, and sometimes Romani people, into small sections of towns and cities, furthering their exploitation.

**partisan*: A member of an irregular military force formed to oppose control of an area by a foreign power, or by an army of occupation, by some kind of insurgent activity. The term can apply to the field element of resistance movements, examples of which are the civilians who opposed Nazi German, Fascist Italian, and Ustaše Croatian rule in several countries during World War II.

12
S'dremlen feygl oyf di tsvaygn

sdrɛm.lɜn   fɛɪ.gl̩   ʔɔɪf   di   tsvaɪ.gn̩
S'dremlen   **feygl**   **oyf**   **di**   **tsvaygn**
There doze   birds   on   the   branches

Words: Leah Rudnicki (1916-1943)
Music: Leyb Yampolski (dates unknown)

TEXT:
- IPA Transliteration
- **Sung Text**
- Word-for-Word Translation

| **IDIOMATIC TRANSLATION** |

---

sdrɛm.lɜn   fɛɪ.gl̩   ʔɔɪf   di   tsvaɪ.gn̩
S'dremlen   feygl   oyf   di   tsvaygn;
There doze   birds   on   the   branches

ʃlɔf   maɪn   taɪ.ɜʃ   kɪnd
Shlof,   mayn   tayer   kind.
Sleep   my   dear   child

baɪ   daɪn   vi.gl̩   ʔɔɪf   daɪn   na.ɾɜ
Bay   dayn   vigl,   oyf   dayn   nare,
By   your   cradle   in   your   nest

zɪtst   ʔa   frɛm.dɜ   ʔʊn   zɪŋt
Zitst   a   fremde   un   zingt
Sits   a   stranger   and   sings

lu   lu lu   lu lu
Lu - lu, lu - lu, lu
Lu   lu lu   lu lu

> Birds sit dozing on the branches;
> Sleep, my precious child.
> By your cradle, in your lair,
> Sings a stranger by your side.
> Lu-lu, lu-lu, lu…

---

sɪz   daɪn   vi.gl̩   vu   gɜ.'ʃta.nɜn
S'iz   dayn   vigl   vu   geshtanen,
It is   your   cradle   where   stood

'ɔɪs.gɜ.flɔx.tn̩   fʊn   glik
Oysgeflokhtn   fun   glik;
Woven   with   joy

ʊn   daɪn   ma.mɜ   ʔɔɪ   daɪn   ma.mɜ
Un   dayn   mame,   oy   dayn   mame,
And   your   mother   oh   your   mother

kumt   ʃɔɪn   kɛɪn   mɔl   nɪt   tsu.ɾɪk
Kumt   shoyn   keyn   mol   nit   tsurik.
Comes   already   no   time   not   back

lu   lu lu   lu lu
Lu - lu, lu - lu, lu

> Here stands your cradle,
> Woven with joy,
> And your mother, oh your mother,
> Is never coming back.
> Lu-lu, lu-lu, lu…(etc.)

---

xhɔb   gɜ.'zɛɪn   daɪn   ta.tn̩   lɔɪ.fn̩
Kh'hob   gezeyn   dayn   tatn   loyfn
I have   seen   your   father running

ʊn.tɜʃ   hɔ.gl̩   fʊn   ʃtɛɪn
Unter   hogl   fun   shteyn;
Under   (a)hail   of   stones

i.bɜʃ   fɛl.dɜʃ   ʔɪz   gɜ.'flɔɪ.gn̩
Iber   felder   iz   gefloygn,
Over   fields   has   flown

zaɪn   faɾ.'jɔ.sɛm.tɜʃ   gɜ.'vɛɪn
Zayn   faryosemter   geveyn.
His   desolate   moaning

lu   lu lu   lu lu
Lu - lu, lu - lu, lu

> I saw your father running
> Under a hail of stones;
> Across the fields flew
> His desolate moaning.
> Lu-lu, lu-lu, lu…(etc.)

12
S'dremlen feygl oyf di tsvaygn

Words by Leah Rudnicki (1916-1943)
Music by Leyb Yampolski (dates unknown)

Arrangement by Robert De Cormier
(piano reduction by John Yaffé)

Andante moderato (♩ = ca. 62-66)

a tempo

mf dreamily

S'drem-len fey - gl oyf di tsvay - gn;

Shlof, mayn ta - yer___ kind. Bay___ dayn vi - gl, oyf dayn na - re,

p espr.

zitst a frem - de un zingt. Bay___ dayn vi - gl, oyf dayn na - re,

11

zitst a frem - de un zingt: Lu - lu, lu - lu,

poco rit. *a tempo* *poco rit.* *a tempo* *rit.*

15

lu._____ S'iz dayn vi - gl

B **Poco più mosso** (♩= ca. 88-96)

mf

19

vu ge - shta - nen, oys - ge - flokh - tn fun glik;_____ Un__ dayn ma - me,

Tempo I (♩= ca. 62-66)

p

23

oy dayn ma - me, kumt shoyn keyn mol nit tsu - rik._____ Un__ dayn ma - me,

espr.

oy dayn ma - me, kumt shoyn keyn mol nit tsu - rik. Lu - lu, lu -

lu, lu.

Kh'hob ge - zeyn dayn ta - tn loy - fn un - ter ho - gl fun shteyn;___

I - ber fel - der iz ge - floy - gn, zayn far - yo - sem - ter ge - veyn.__

S'dremlen feygl oyf di tsvaygn

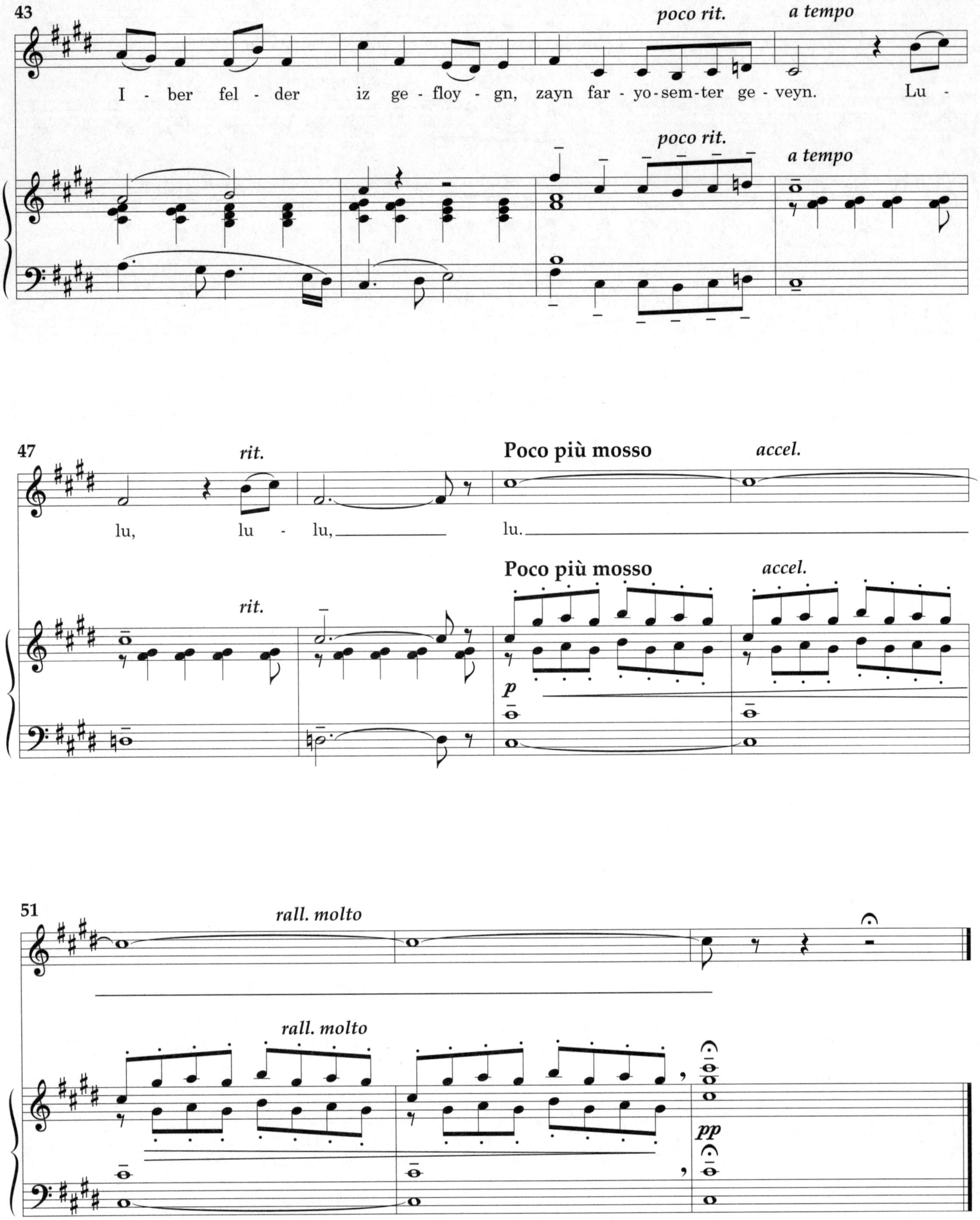
43
poco rit.
a tempo
I - ber fel - der iz ge - floy - gn, zayn far - yo-sem-ter ge - veyn. Lu -
poco rit.
a tempo
47
rit.
Poco più mosso
accel.
lu, lu - lu,
lu.
Poco più mosso
accel.
rit.
p
51
rall. molto
rall. molto
pp

13
Sheyn bin ikh, sheyn

This song is an example of a song that little girls might have sung as they acted out the traditional Jewish wedding. A wedding match ('shidikhim') with a rabbinical scholar was considered most fortuitous, and supporting a husband in his study of the *Torah** was an honoured vocation for a wife.

According to Ruth Rubin:

> Marriage was the high point in the life of the young boy or girl of that day, and Jewish folklore is replete with references to the wedding day, the preparations for it, the ceremony, and the relationship between the families. Children skipped to rhymes that spoke of marriage. Parents dangled their children on their knees, singing about their future happiness and the security of a good match. Such is this little skipping song.

Torah: Torah ('Instruction', 'Teaching', or 'Law') has a range of meanings. It can most specifically mean the first five books (*Pentateuch*) of the twenty-four books of the Hebrew Bible and it is usually printed with rabbinic commentary; it can mean the continued narrative from the Book of Genesis to the end of the Hebrew Bible; and it can even mean the totality of Jewish teaching, culture and practice, whether derived from biblical texts or later rabbinic writings.

13

Sheyn bin ikh, sheyn

ʃɛɪn	bɪn	ʔɪx	ʃɛɪn
Sheyn	**bin**	**ikh,**	**sheyn**
Pretty	am	I,	pretty

(Anonymous)

TEXT:
- IPA Transliteration
- **Sung Text**
- Word-for-Word Translation

IDIOMATIC TRANSLATION

ʃɛɪn	bɪn	ʔɪx	ʃɛɪn	ʃɛɪn	ʔɪz	maɪn	na.mɜn
Sheyn	**bin**	**ikh,**	**sheyn,**	**sheyn**	**iz**	**mayn**	**namen;**
Pretty	am	I	pretty	pretty	is	my	name

rɛt	mɛn	mɪr	ʃɪ.'di.xɪm		fʊn	sa.mɜ	ra.'bɔ.nɪm
Redt	**men**	**mir**	**shidikhim**		**fun**	**same**	**rabonim.**
Talk	one	to me	marriage match		of	actual	Rabbi

ra.'bɔ.nɪ.ʃɜ	tɔɪ.rɜ	ʔɪz	dɔx	zɛɪ.ɜr	grɔɪs
Rabonishe	**toyre**	**iz**	**dokh**	**zeyer**	**groys;**
Rabbinic	Torah	is	yes	very	great

bɪn	ʔɪx	baɪ	maɪn	ma.mɜn	ʔa	'lɪx.tɪ.gɜ	rɔɪz
Bin	**ikh**	**bay**	**mayn**	**mamen**	**a**	**likhtige**	**royz.**
Am	I	to	my	mother	a	bright	rose

Pretty am I, pretty,
'Pretty' is my name.
They talk to me of a match
With an actual rabbi!
Rabbinic learning
Is very important;
And in my mother's eye,
I am a radiant rose.

a	ʃɛɪn	'mɛɪ.dɜ.lɜ	bɪn	ʔɪx	rɔɪ.tɜ	'zɛ.kɜ.lɜx	trɔg	ʔɪx
A	**sheyn**	**meydele**	**bin**	**ikh,**	**royte**	**zekelekh**	**trog**	**ikh;**
A	pretty	girl	am	I	red	stockings	wear	I

gɛlt	ʔɪn	di	ta.ʃn̩	vaɪn	ʔɪn	di	fla.ʃn̩
Gelt	**in**	**di**	**tashn,**	**vayn**	**in**	**di**	**flashn.**
Money	in	the	pockets	wine	in	the	bottles

mi.lɜx	ʔɪn	di	'kri.gɜ.lɜx	kɪn.dɜr	ʔɪn	di	'vi.gɜ.lɜx
Milekh	**in**	**di**	**krigelekh,**	**kinder**	**in**	**di**	**vigelekh**
Mead	in	the	crocks	children	in	the	cradle

ʃraɪn	ʔa.lɜ	ʃɛɪn	ʃɛɪn	bɪn	ʔɪx	ʃɛɪn
Shrayn	**ale,**	**"Sheyn!"**	**Sheyn**	**bin**	**ikh,**	**sheyn.**
Shout	all	pretty	pretty	am	I	pretty

A pretty girl am I,
I wear red stockings,
I have money in my pockets,
I have wine in the bottles,
I have mead in the crocks,
Children in the cradle.
All cry out, "Pretty!"
Pretty am I, pretty.

bɛ.sɜr	ʔa	mɜ.'la.mɜd	ʔa.'fi.lɜ	ʔa	bɛɪ.zn̩
Besser	**a**	**melamed,**	**afile**	**a**	**beyzn,**
Better	a	tutor	even	a	mean one

ɛɪ.dɜr	ʔa	ʃtu.'dɜnt	mɪt	tsɜ.'rɪ.sɜ.nɜ	hɛɪ.zn̩
Eyder	**a**	**shtudent**	**mit**	**tserisene**	**heyzn;**
Before	a	student	with	torn	trousers

bɛ.sɜr	ʔa	ba.'hɛl.fɜr	mɪt	a	tuts	klɛɪ.nɜ	kɪn.dɜr
Besser	**a**	**bahelfer**	**mit**	**a**	**tuts**	**kleyne**	**kinder**
Better	a	tutor	with	a	dozen	small	children

ɛɪ.dɜr	gɔr	ʔa	dɔk.tɜr	mɪt	a	tsɜ.'brɔx.ɜn.ɜm	tsɪ.'lɪn.dɜr
Eyder	**gor**	**a**	**dokter**	**mit**	**a**	**tsebrokhenem**	**tsilinder.**
Before	even	a	doctor	with	a	broken	cylinder hat

Better a tutor,
Even a mean one,
Than a student
With torn trousers.
Better a teacher's helper
With twelve kids of his own
Than a doctor
With a broken top hat.

a	ʃɛɪn	'mɛɪ.dɜ.lɜ	bɪn	ʔɪx
A	**sheyn**	**meydele**	**bin**	**ikh…(etc.)**
A	pretty	girl	am	I

A pretty girl am I…(etc.)

bɛ.sɜɾ a pɾɔs.tɜɾ klɔɪz.nɪk   ʔa.'fi.lɜ nɪt kɛin gʊ.tɜɾ
Besser a proster kloyznik,   afile nit keyn guter,
Better a plain yeshiva student even not no good one

ɛi.dɜɾ ʔan ap.'tɛ.kɜɾ vɔs pɾɛ.gɜlt flɛiʃ ʔɔif pʊ.tɜɾ
Eyder an apteker vos pregelt fleysh oyf puter;
Before an apothecary who fries meat in butter

ɪx vɪl nɛ.mɜn ʔa xɔ.sɪd mɪt a pɔr laŋ.gɜ pɛ.ɜs
Ikh vil nemen a khosid mit a por lange peyes,
I want (to)marry a Chasid with a pair long earlocks

ʊn ʔɛɾ vɛt mɪr fɛŋ.gɜn fʊn ʔʊnd.zɜɾ ɾɛ.bn̩ ka.'mɛ.ɜs
Un er vet mir fengen fun undzer rebn kameyes.
And he will me bring from our rebbe (lucky)charms

Better a plain old yeshiva boy,
Even if he's not so bright,
Than an apothecary
Who fries meat in butter.
I'll take a Chasid
With a pair of long earlocks,
And he'll get childbirth charms
For me from the rebbe.

a ʃɛɪn 'mɛi.dʒ.lɜ bɪn ʔɪx
A sheyn meydele bin ikh…(etc.)
A pretty girl am I

A pretty girl am I…(etc.)

'Life is no more than a dream — but don't wake me up'
('Dos lebn iz nit mer vi a kholem — ober vek mikh nit oyf')

– Yiddish proverb

13
Sheyn bin ikh, sheyn
(Anonymous)

Arrangement by Robert De Cormier
(piano reduction by John Yaffé)

Lyrics:
Sheyn bin ikh, sheyn, sheyn iz mayn na-men;

redt men mir shi-di-khim fun sa-me ra-bo-nim. Ra-bo-ni-she toy-re iz dokh ze - yer groys; __ bin ikh bay mayn ma - men a likh - ti - ge

B **Più mosso, lively** (♩ = ca. 132)

royz. A sheyn mey-de - le bin ikh, roy - te ze - ke-lekh trog ikh;

gelt in di ta - shn, vayn in di fla - shn. Mi - lekh in di kri - ge-lekh,

(2nd time to ⊕)

kin-der in di vi - ge-lekh. Shrayn a - le, "Sheyn!" Sheyn bin ikh, sheyn.

(2nd time to ⊕)

33
Tempo I (♩ = ca. 126)
Tempo I (♩ = ca. 126)
p
39
C
Calmer (♩ = 100-112)
Be - ser a me - la - med, a - fi - le a bey - zn, ey - der a shtu - dent mit tse -
Calmer (♩ = 100-112)
p
45
accel. poco a poco
ri - se - ne hey - zn; Be - ser a be - hel - fer mit a tuts kley - ne
accel. poco a poco
50
(accel. poco a poco)
kin - der ey - der gor a dok - ter mit a tse - bro - khe - nem tse - lin - der.
(accel. poco a poco)

D **Andante calmo** ($\textbf{.}$ = 94-96)

Be - ser a pros - ter kloyz - nik, a - fi - le nit keyn gu - ter, ey - der an ap -

te - ker vos pre - gelt fleysh oyf pu - ter; Ikh vil ne - men a kho - sid

mit a por lan - ge pey - es, un er vet mir fen - gen fun und - zer re - bn ka -

75
accel. un poco
E
Poco più mosso (♩ = 112-120)
me - yes. A sheyn mey-de - le bin ikh, roy - te ze - ke-lekh trog ikh;
accel. un poco
Poco più mosso (♩ = 112-120)
mf
80
accel. poco a poco
gelt in di ta - shn, vayn in di fla - shn. Mi - lekh in di
accel. poco a poco
85
kri - ge - lekh. Kin-der in di vi - ge - lekh shrayn a - le, "Sheyn!" Sheyn bin ikh,
91
Lively (♩ = ca. 132)
sheyn.
Lively (♩ = ca. 132)

14
Tayere Malke
(or 'Der bekher')

There is a relative dearth of drinking songs in popular Jewish culture. However, one example of a Yiddish folk song that deals with drinking is 'Tayere Malke'. The original words and melody are by folk poet Mark Varshofsky (1840-1907), author and composer of many popular Yiddish songs such as 'Oyfn pripetshik' ('At the Fireplace') and 'De mizinke oysgegebn' ('The Youngest Daughter's Wedding'). The melody was later used for Yosi Kotler's song 'Simkhe mit zayn yidene' ('Simkhe and His Wife'). A second melody was published in 1926 in *90 gekilbene yidishe folkslider*. The current (Robert De Cormier) arrangement, originally done for singer Marthe Schlamme, combines the two melodies into a strophic recitative-/verse-with-chorus structure.

The singing of this song has become a common occurrence at annual Jewish *Passover seders*,* at the point in which the second cup of wine is lifted. The name 'Malke' means 'Queen' and is used as a general term of endearment. However, as tradition has it, the hostess of the Passover seder is 'a queen'. In the course of the song, the persona of the song becomes a bit inebriated — or, as it is said in Yiddish, 'a bissl shiker'.

* *Passover seder*: A Jewish ritual feast that marks the beginning of the Jewish holiday of Passover. It is conducted throughout the world on the evening of the fourteenth day of Nisan in the Hebrew calendar. The ritual is performed by a community, or by multiple generations of a family, and involves a retelling of the story of the liberation of the Israelites from slavery in ancient Egypt (told in the Book of Exodus in The Hebrew Bible).

14

Tayere Malke
(or 'Der bekher')

'taɪ.ɜ.ɾɜ   mal.kɜ   (dɛɾ bɛxɜɾ)
Tayere   Malke (or **Der   bekher**)
Dear   Malke

Words: Mark Varshovsky (1840-1907)
Music: Anonymous

TEXT:
- IPA Transliteration
- **Sung Text**
- Word-for-Word Translation

IDIOMATIC TRANSLATION

'taɪ.ɜ.ɾɜ   mal.kɜ   gɜ.'zʊnt   zols.tu   zaɪn
Tayere   Malke — gezunt   zolstu   zayn!
Dear   Malke   healthy   should you   be

gis   ʔɔn   dɛm   bɛ.xɜɾ   dɛm   bɛ.xɜɾ   mit   vaɪn
Gis   on   dem   bekher,   dem   bekher   mit   vayn.
Pour   in   the   goblet   the   goblet   with   wine

My dear Malke, may you be well!
Fill up the goblet with wine.

jʊm   daɪ   di   dʊm   ba   jʊm   baɪ   di   daɪ
Yum   day   di   dum   ba,   yum   bay   di   day…(etc.)
Yum   day   di   dum   ba   yum   bay   di   dai

Yum day di dum ba, yum bay di dai

fʊn   dɛm   'dɔ.zɪ.kn̩   bɛ.xɜɾ   vɔs   glantst   ʔa.'zɔɪ   ʃeɪn
Fun   dem   dozikn   bekher, vos   glantst   azoy   sheyn,
From the   this   goblet   that   shines   so   beautifully

hɔt   gɜ.'trʊŋ.kɜn   maɪn   zeɪ.dɜ   maɪn   zeɪ.dɜ   ʔa.'leɪn
Hot   getrunken   mayn   zeyde,   mayn   zeyde   aleyn.
Has   drunk   my   grandpa   my   grandpa   himself

gɜ.'vɛn   ʃlɛx.tɜ   tsaɪ.tn̩   vi   ʔɛs   maxt   zix   ʔa.'mɔl
Geven   shlekhte tsaytn, vi   es   makht   zikh   amol;
There were   bad   times   as   it   does   itself   sometimes

nɔɾ   dɛm   bɛx.ɜɾ   hɔt   ʔɛɾ   gɜ.'hal.tn̩   ʔaɪ.zn̩ ʔʊn   ʃtɔl
Nor   dem   bekher hot   er   gehaltn —   ayzn   un   shtol.
But   the   goblet   has   he   held   iron   and   steel

From this goblet,
Which gleams so beautifully,
My grandfather would drink,
My grandfather himself.
There have been bad times,
As sometimes happen;
But he clung to the goblet
Like iron and steel.

jʊm   daɪ   di   dʊm   ba
Yum   day   di   dum   ba…(etc.)

Yum dai dee dum ba…(etc.)

'taɪ.ɜ.ɾɜ   mal.kɜ   gɜ.'zʊnt   zɔls.tu   zaɪn
Tayere   Malke —   gezunt   zolstu   zayn!
Dear   Malke   healthy   should you   be

faɾ   vɛ.mɜn zɔl   ʔɪx   trɪŋ.kɜn   dɛm   'dɔ.zɪ.kn̩ vaɪn
Far   vemen zol   ikh   trinken, dem   dozikn   vayn?
For   whom   should   I   drink   the   this   wine

ʊn   mɪɾ   vɛ.ln̩   trɪŋ.kɜn? ʊn   gɔɾ   ʔɔn   an   ʔɛk
Un   mir   veln   trinken   un   gor   on   an   ek
And   we   will   drink   and   completely without   an   end

faɾ   di   vɔs   zaɪ.nɜn   fʊn   ʊnz   ɔɪf   ɛɪ.bɪk   a.vɛk
Far   di   vos   zaynen   fun   unz   oyf   eybik   avek!
For   those   who   are   of   us   forever   gone!

My dear Malke, may you be well!
For whom shall I drink this wine?
We shall drink, and drink without end,
To those of us who have departed!

jʊm   daɪ   di   dʊm   ba
Yum   day   di   dum   ba,…(etc.)

lɜ.xa.jim
L'khayim!
To life!

Yum dai dee dum ba…(etc.)
To life!

14
Tayere Malke
(or 'Der bekher')

Words by Mark Varshofsky (1840-1907)
(to an anonymous folk song)

Arrangement by Robert De Cormier
(piano reduction by John Yaffé)

Lyrics (vocal line):

Ta - ye - re Mal - ke, ge -

zundt zols-tu zayn! Gis — on dem be - kher, dem be - kher mit vayn! —

Yum day di dum ba, yum bay di day; Yum bay di

12
di da da, ay ay ay ay di di di di di. Yum day di dum ba,
mf
17
stentato
yum bay di day; Yum bay di di da da, ay ay ay ay.
stentato
23
Moderato
rit.
Andante
B
as before
Fun dem do - zi - kn
(mf)
p
col canto
27
Andante (in 4)
be - kher, vos glantst a - zoy sheyn, hot ge - trun - ken mayn zey - de, mayn

zey - de a-leyn. Ge - ven shlekh - te tsay - tn, vi es makht zikh a - mol; Nur dem

be-kher hot er ge-hal - tn — ay - zn un shtol!__ Yum day di dum ba,

yum bay di day; Yum bay di di da da, ay ay ay

ay di di di di di. Yum day di dum ba, yum bay di day;

Tayere Malke

50
stentato
54
Yum bay di di da da, ay ay ay ay.
stentato
(mf)
55
Moderato
rit.
Andante
D
as before
Ta - ye - re Mal - ke, ge - zundt zols - tu
mf
p
col canto
60
Andante (in 4)
as before
zayn! Far ve - men zol ikh trin - ken, dem do - zi - kn vayn? Un mir vi - len
col canto
64
Andante (in 4)
trin - ken un gor on an ek far di vos zay - nen fun unz oyf
mf

* 'L'khayim! ' = ' To life! '
N.B. Yiddish takes the word 'khay' ('life') and doubles it with the plural Hebrew ending '-im',
so that all will be blessed with twice as much as expected!

Tayere Malke

15
Tum-balalayke

This song is one of the most popular of all Yiddish love songs. The music is cast in the form of a waltz, the words cast in the form of a riddle, with 'Tum-balalayke'* as the refrain.

This is a traditional Yiddish song about a boy who wants to get married, but he can't decide to *whom*. He is a smart boy, he wants to choose a smart girl, and, at the same time, he doesn't want to shame anyone by shunning them. So, he stays up late at night inventing riddles to test his potential bride(s).

* 'Tum' is the Yiddish word for 'noise', and a *balalayke* is a stringed musical instrument of Russian origin.

15
Tum-balalayke

tʊm   ba.la.ˈlai.kɜ
Tum - balalayke

(Anonymous)

TEXT:
- IPA Transliteration
- **Sung Text**
- Word-for-Word Translation

IDIOMATIC TRANSLATION

---

tʊm   ba.la   tʊm ba.la   tʊm ba.la.ˈlai.kɜ
Tum - bala,   tum-bala,   tum-balalayke.
Tum - bala   tum-bala   tum-balalayke

tʊm   ba.la.ˈlai.kɜ   shpil   ba.la.ˈlai.kɜ
Tum - balalayke,   shpil   balalayke,
Tum - balalayke   play   balalayke

tʊm   ba.la.ˈlai.kɜ   fɾɛɪ.lɜx   zɔl   zaɪn
Tum - balalayke,   freylekh zol   zayn
Tum - balalayke   joyful   should be

Tum-bala, tum-bala, tum-balalayke.
Tum-bala, tum-bala, tum-balalayke.
Tum-balalayke, play, balalayke,
Tum-balalayke — Play something merry!

ʃtɛɪt   ʔa   bɔx.ɜɾ   ʔʊn   ʔɛɾ   tɾaxt
Shteyt   a   bokher   un   er   trakht,
Stands   a   boy   and he ponders

tɾaxt   ʔʊn   tɾaxt   ʔa   gan.tsɜ   naxt
Trakht   un   trakht   a   gantse   nakht:
Ponders   and ponders a   whole   night

vɛ.mɜn   tsu   nɛ.mɜn ʔʊn   nit   faɾ.ˈʃɛ.mɜn
Vemen   tsu   nemen   un   nit farshemen,
Who   to   marry   and not shame

Tum - bala,   tum-bala,   tum-balalayke…(etc.)

There stands a boy, and he ponders;
Ponders and ponders, the whole night through:
Whom he should marry and not put to shame,
Whom he should marry and not put to shame.
Tum-bala, tum-bala, tum-balalayke…(etc.)

mɛɪ.dl̩   mɛɪ.dl̩   xvɛl   baɪ dɪɾ fɾɛgn̩
"Meydl,   meydl,   kh'vel bay dir fregn:
Maiden   maiden   I will   by you ask

vɔs   kɛn vak.sn̩ vak.sn̩ ʔɔn   ɾɛgn̩
Vos   ken vaksn,   vaksn   on   regn?
What can   grow   grow   without rain

vɔs   kɛn bɾɛ.nɜn   ʔʊn   nit   ˈʔɔɪf.hɛɾn̩
Vos   ken brenen   un   nit   oyfhern?
What can   burn   and not   cease

vɔs   kɛn bɛŋ.kɜn   vɛɪ.nɜn ʔɔn   tɾɛɾn̩
Vos   ken benken,   veynen on   trern?"
What can   yearn   cry   without tears

Tum - bala,   tum-bala,   tum-balalayke…(etc.)

"Maiden, maiden, I'll ask you this:
What can grow without rain?
What can burn without end?
What can yearn, cry without tears?"
Tum-bala, tum-bala, tum-balalayke…(etc.)

ˈna.ɾɪ.ʃɜɾ   bɔx.ɜɾ   vɔs   daɾfs.tu fɾɛgn̩
"Narisher   bokher,   vos   darfstu fregn?
Foolish   boy   what may you ask

a ʃtɛɪn   kɛn vak.sn̩ vak.sn̩ ʔɔn   ɾɛgn̩
A shteyn   ken vaksn,   vaksn   on   regn.
A stone   can grow   grow   without rain

a li.bɜ   kɛn bɾɛ.nɜn   ʔʊn   nit   ˈʔɔɪ.fhɛɾn̩
A libe   ken brenen   un   nit   oyfhern.
A love   can burn   and not   cease

a haɾts   kɛn bɛŋ.kɜn   vɛɪ.nɜn ʔɔn   tɾɛɾn̩
A harts   ken benken,   veynen on   trern."
A heart   can yearn   cry   without   tears

Tum - bala,   tum-bala,   tum-balalayke…(etc.)

"Foolish boy, how can you even ask!
A stone can grow without rain;
Love can burn without end;
A heart can yearn and cry without tears."
Tum-bala, tum-bala, tum-balalayke…(etc.)

15
Tum-balalayke
(Anonymous)

Arrangement by Robert De Cormier
(piano reduction by John Yaffé)

'Ländler' tempo (♩. = ca. 52)

Tum - ba - la, tum - ba - la,

tum - ba - la - lay - ke. Tum - ba - la, tum - ba - la, tum - ba - la -

lay - ke, Tum - ba - la - lay - ke, shpil, ba - la - lay - ke,

116

Tum-balalayke

Tum-balalayke

Tum-balalayke

Tum-balalayke

92
F
Na - ri - sher bo - kher, vos darfs - tu fregn? A shteyn ken
p
espr.
98
vak - sn, vak - sn on regn; A li - be ken bre - - nen
103
poco a poco rit.
un nit oyf - hern; A harts ken ben - ken, vey - nen on
poco a poco rit.
108
a tempo
G
trern. Tum - ba - la, tum - ba - la, tum - ba - la - lay - - ke.
a tempo
mf
p

Tum-balalayke

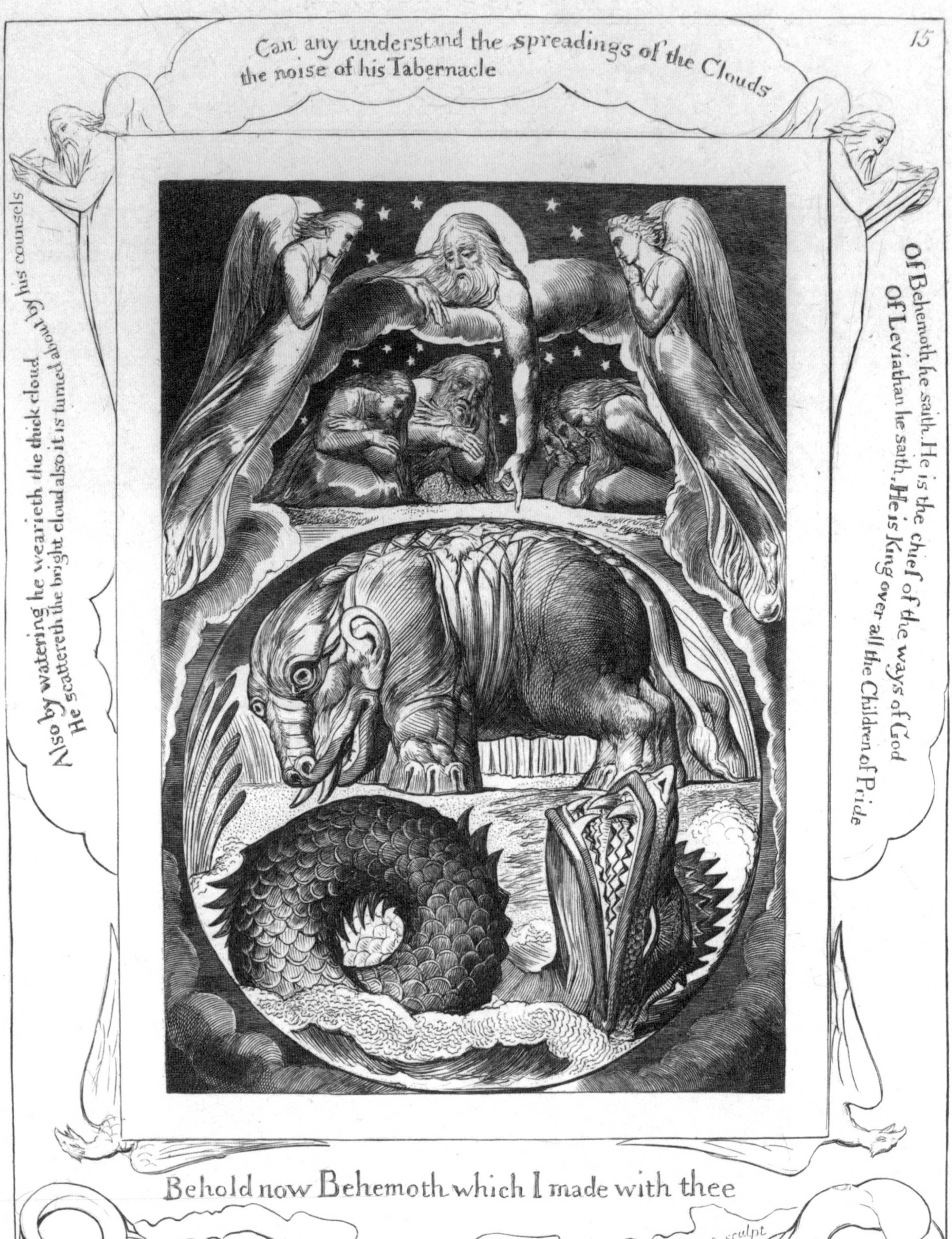
15
Can any understand the spreadings of the Clouds
the noise of his Tabernacle
Also by watering he wearieth the thick cloud
He scattereth the bright cloud also it is turned about by his counsels
Of Behemoth he saith. He is the chief of the ways of God
Of Leviathan he saith. He is King over all the Children of Pride
Behold now Behemoth which I made with thee
W Blake invenit & sculpt
London. Published as the Act directs March 8. 1825 by Will Blake N3 Fountain Court Strand

Above image: William Blake, from his illustrations of the *Book of Job*.

16
Vos vet zayn az Meshiakh vet kumen? (or 'Zog zhe, rebenyu')

The term *Messiah (Meshiakh)* — literally meaning somebody who has been 'annointed' in an act of ritual consecration — has come to refer specifically to a future Jewish king from the *Davidic line,** who will rule the Jewish people during the Messianic Age.** When the Messiah comes, the righteous will sit down to a meal of Leviathan (biblical sea monster), Wild Ox, and Preserved Wine, each one of these constituents hailing from the six days of creation of the world and abounding in symbolic significance. According to midrashim (biblical exegesis by ancient Judaic authorities, prominent in the *Talmud***), the wine preserved from Creation symbolizes the Torah, while the Wild Ox (symbol of the revealed tradition of the Torah) and Leviathan (symbol of 'the concealed realm') will battle and defeat each other, and at the 'End of Days'**** be served to the 'righteous' at the 'Heavenly Feast'.

Folklorist Ruth Rubin writes:

> I received my Jewish education in the home and in a secular school, which taught Yiddish and Hebrew and the stories of the Bible, as well as singing in both languages. The Sabbath (every week) and the holidays were marked by stories, games, plays, and walks in nature. This 'cumulative song' was a favorite at birthday parties and social gatherings.

* *Davidic line*: This refers to the tracing of lineage to King David through the texts in the Hebrew Bible, in the New Testament, and through the succeeding centuries.

** *Messianic Age*: In Abrahamic religions, the Messianic Age is the future period of time on Earth in which the messiah will reign and bring universal peace and brotherhood, a time devoid of evil. Many believe that there will be such an age; some refer to it as the consummate 'kingdom of God' or the 'world to come'.

*** *Talmud*: The central text of Rabbinic Judaism and the primary source of Jewish religious law and Jewish theology.

**** *End of Days*: a future time-period described variously in the eschatologies of several world religions (both Abrahamic and non-Abrahamic), which teach that world events will reach a final climax.

16
Vos vet zayn az
Meshiakh vet kumen?
(or 'Zog zhe, rebenyu')

vɔs vɛt zaɪn ʔaz mɜ.ˈʃi.ax vɛt kʊ.mɜn
Vos vet zayn az Meshiakh vet kumen?
What will be when Messiah will come

(Anonymous)

TEXT:
- IPA Transliteration
- Sung Text
- Word-for-Word Translation

IDIOMATIC TRANSLATION

---

zɔg ʒʒ ʔʊndz ˈɾɛ.bɜ.nju
Zog zhe undz rebenyu:
Tell then us Rabbi

vɔs vɛt zaɪn ʔaz mɜ.ˈʃi.ax vɛt kʊ.mɜn
Vos vet zayn, az Meshiakh vet kumen?
What will be when Messiah will come

az mɜ.ˈʃiax vɛt kʊ.mɜn
"Az Meshiakh vet kumen,
When Messiah will come

vɛln mɪɾ ma.xn̩ ʔa ˈsu.dɜ.nju
veln mir makhn a sude-nyu."
Will we make a feast

Tell us, Rebbe:
What will happen when the Messiah comes?
"When the Messiah comes,
There will be a great feast."

vɔs vɛln mɪɾ ʔɛ.sn̩ ʔɔɪf dɛɾ ˈsu.dɜ.nju
Vos veln mir esn oyf der sude-nyu?
What will we eat at the feast

dɛm ˈʃɔɾ.ha.bɔɾ mɪtn lɛv.ˈjɔ.sn̩
"Dem shorhabor mitn levyosn,
The Wild Ox with a Leviathan

dɛm ˈʃɔɾ.ha.bɔɾ mɪtn lɛv.ˈjɔ.sn̩ vɛln mɪɾ ʔɛ.sn̩
Dem shorhabor mitn levyosn veln mir esn...
The Wild Ox with the Leviathan will we eat

ɔɪf dɛɾ ˈsu.dɜ.nju
oyf der sude-nyu!"
at the feast

What will we eat at this feast?
"The Wild Ox and the Leviathan,
The Wild Ox and the Leviathan;
The Wild Ox and the Leviathan
Is what we'll eat at the feast!"

vɔs vɛln mɪɾ tɾɪŋ.kɜn ʔɔɪf dɛɾ ˈsu.dɜ.nju
Vos veln mir trinken oyf der sude-nyu?
What will we drink at the feast

ja.jɪn ham.ˈʃʊ.mɜɾ ja.jɪn ham.ˈʃʊ.mɜɾ
"Yayin hamshumer, yayin hamshumer;
(the)Wine of Creation wine of Creation

ɔɪ ja.jɪn ham.ˈʃʊ.mɜɾ
Oy, yayin hamshumer...(etc.)"
Ah, wine of Creation

What will we drink at this feast?
"Wine from the six days of Creation;
Wine from the days of Creation
Is what we'll drink,
The Wild Ox and the Leviathan
Is what we'll eat...(etc.)"

vɛɾ vɛt ʔʊndz tɔɪ.ɾɜ zɔ.gn̩ ʔɔɪf dɛɾ ˈsu.dɜ.nju
Ver vet undz toyre zogn oyf der sude-nyu?
Who will us Torah teach at the feast

mɔɪ.ʃɜ ɾa.ˈbɛ.nju mɔɪ.ʃɜ ɾa.ˈbɛ.nju
"Moyshe rabenyu, Moyshe rabenyu;
Moses our teacher Moses our teacher

ɔɪ mɔɪ.ʃɜ ɾa.ˈbɛ.nju vɛt ʔʊndz tɔɪ.ɾɜ zɔ.gn̩
Oy, Moyshe rabenyu vet undz toyre zogn,
Ah, Moses our teacher will us Torah teach

ja.jɪn ham.ˈʃʊ.mɜɾ
yayin hamshumer...(etc.)"
wine of Creation

Who will teach Torah to us at this feast?
"Moses, our teacher, Moses, our teacher;
Moses, our teacher, will teach us Torah,
Wine from the days of Creation
Is what we'll drink...(etc.)"

vɛɾ vɛt ʔʊndz ʃpi.ln̩ ʔɔɪf dɛɾ 'su.dɛ.nju
Ver vet undz shpiln oyf der sude-nyu?
Who will (to)us play at the feast

dɔ.vɪd ha.'mɛɪ.lɛx dɔ.vɪd ha.'mɛɪ.lɛx
"Dovid hameylekh, Dovid hameylekh;
David the King David the King

ɔɪ dɔ.vɪd ha.'mɛɪ.lɛx vɛt ʔʊndz ʃpi.ln̩
Oy, Dovid hameylekh vet undz shpiln,
Ah David the King will to us play

mɔɪ.ʃɜ ɾa.'bɛ.nju
Moyshe rabenyu…(etc.)"
Moses our teacher

Who will play for us at this feast?
"King David, King David;
King David will play for us,
Moses, our teacher, will teach us Torah…(etc.)"

vɛɾ vɛt ʔʊndz tan.tsn̩ ʔɔɪf dɛɾ 'su.dɜ.nju
Ver vet undz tantsn oyf der sude-nyu?
Who will to us dance at the feast?

'mi.ɾi.am ha.nɛ.'vi.a 'mi.ɾi.am ha.nɛ.'vi.a
"Miriam hanevia, Miriam hanevia;
Miriam Prophetess Miriam Prophetess

ɔɪ miɾ.iam ha.nɛ.'vi.a vɛt ʔʊndz tan.tsn̩
Oy, Miriam haneviya vet undz tantsn,
Ah, Miriam (the)Prophetess will to us dance

dɔ.vɪd ha.'mɛɪ.lɛx
Dovid hameylekh…(etc.)"
David the King

Who will dance for us at this feast?
"Miriam the Prophetess, Miriam the Prophetess;
Miriam the Prophetess will dance for us,
King David will play for us…(etc.)"

16
Vos vet zayn az Meshiakh vet kumen?
(or 'Zog zhe, rebenyu')

(Anonymous)

Arrangement by Robert De Cormier
(piano reduction by John Yaffé)

Lyrics:

Zog zhe undz re-be-nyu: Vos vet zayn, az Me-shi-akh vet ku-men? "Az Me-shi-akh vet ku-men, veln mir ma-khn a su-den-

5
B
ten.
yu." Vos veln mir e - sn oyf der su - den - yu? "Dem
f
ped.
7
Poco adagio (♩ = ca. 60)
shor ha - bor mitn lev - yo - - - sn, dem shor ha - bor mitn lev - yo - - - sn; Dem
Poco adagio (♩ = ca. 60)
p
9
Poco più mosso (♩ = ca. 76)
Largo, in 8
shor ha - bor mitn lev - yo - sn veln mir e - sn… oyf der su - den - yu!"
Poco più mosso (♩ = ca. 76)
Largo, in 8
p
p

Vos veln mir trin-ken oyf der su-den-yu? "Ya-yin ham-shu - - - mer,

ya-yin ham-shu - - - mer;___ Oy, ya-yin ham-shu-mer veln mir trin-ken,

shor ha-bor mitn lev-yo - sn veln mir e - sn... oyf der su-den-yu!"___

Vos vet zayn az Meshiakh vet kumen?

Ver vet undz toy-re zo-gn oyf der su-den-yu? "Moy-she ra-be - - -nyu,

Moy-she ra-be - - nyu;__ Oy, Moy-she ra-be-nyu vet undz toy-re zo-gn,

ya-yin ham-shu-mer veln mir trin-ken, shor ha-bor mitn lev-yo-sn veln mir e-sn...

Vos vet zayn az Meshiakh vet kumen?

E
25
Largo, in 8
(a piacere)
oyf der su - den - yu!"
Ver vet undz shpi - - - - - - ln oyf der su-den-yu?
Largo, in 8
p
mf col canto
ten.
a tempo
"Do-vid ha-mey - - - lekh,
a tempo
p
28
a tempo, accel. e cresc. poco a poco
Do-vid ha-mey - - - lekh; Oy, Do-vid ha-mey-lekh vet undz shpi - ln,
a tempo, accel. e cresc. poco a poco

30 Moy - she ra - be - nyu vet undz toy - re zo - gn, ya - yin ham-shu - mer veln mir trin - ken,

32 shor ha - bor mitn lev - yo - sn veln mir e - sn... oyf der su - den - yu!"

Largo, in 8

34 (a piacere) Ver vet undz tan - - - - tsn oyf der su-den-yu? "Mi - ri - am ha - ne - vi - - a,

a tempo col canto

36 Mi - ri - am ha - ne - vi - - a;___ Oy, Mi - riam ha - ne - vi - a vet undz tan - tsn,

a tempo, accel. e cresc. poco a poco

Vos vet zayn az Meshiakh vet kumen?

Vos vet zayn az Meshiakh vet kumen?

17
Zog, maran

This song is a dialogue of two 'Marranos', Spanish Jews who in the early days of the Spanish Inquisition (at the end of the fifteenth century) were forced to embrace the official religion of Christianity but carried on their Jewish traditions in secret. The song evokes the image of such a 'crypto-Jew', who, in post-Expulsion Spain, stubbornly clings to residual *seder** observances, knowing that if caught he could be executed by order of the Inquisition. The poem tells of the character's dedication to his faith, a quiet heroism that can be heard throughout the music as well. Soon after Samuel Bugatch wrote 'Zog, maran' (which is one of his best-known songs), its singing became, in many situations, a regular part of the annual ritual of *Passover*.**

* *seder*: The Jewish ritual service and ceremonial dinner for the first night, or first two nights, of Passover.

** *Passover* (in Hebrew, *Pesakh*) commemorates the exodus of the Jews from slavery in Egypt. The holiday originated in the Torah, where the word pesakh refers to the ancient Passover sacrifice (known as the Paschal Lamb); it is also said to refer to the idea that God 'passed over the houses of the Jews during the 'tenth plague' on the Egyptians: the slaying of the first born. The holiday is ultimately a celebration of freedom, and the story of the exodus from Egypt is a powerful metaphor that is appreciated not only by Jews, but by people of other faiths as well.

17

Zog, maran

zɔg   ma.ˈran
Zog,   maran
Tell,   Marrano

Words: Abraham Reisen (1876-1953)
Music: Samuel Bugatch (1898-1984)

TEXT:
• IPA Transliteration
• **Sung Text**
• Word-for-Word Translation

IDIOMATIC TRANSLATION

---

zɔg   ma.ˈran   du   bɾu.dɚ   mai.nɚ
Zog,   maran,   du   bruder   mayner:
Tell   Marrano   you   bother   mine

vu   ʔiz   gɾɛit   dɛɾ   sɛi.dɚ   dai.nɚ
Vu   iz   greyt   der   seyder   dayner?
Where   is   prepared   your   seder   your

ɪn   ti.fɚ   hɛil   ʔin   a   xɛi.dɚ
"In   tifer   heyl,   in   a   kheyder,
In   deep   cave   in   a   chamber

dɔɾt   hɔb   ʔix   gɜ.ˈgɾɛit   main   sɛi.dɚ
Dort   hob   ikh   gegreyt   mayn   seyder."
There   have   I   prepared   my   seder

Tell me, Marrano, my brother:
Where have you prepared your seder?
"In a chamber in a deep cave,
There I have prepared my seder."

---

zɔg   ma.ˈran   mɪɾ   vu   bai   vɛ.mɜn
Zog,   maran   mir,   vu   bay   vemen,
Tell   Marrano   to me   where   from   whom

vɛs.tu   vai.sɜ   mat.sɜs   nɛ.mɜn
Vestu   vayse   matses   nemen?
Will you   white   matzahs   get

ɪn   dɛɾ   hɛil   ʔɔif   gɔts   ba.ˈɾɔ.tn̩
"In   der   heyl,   oyf   gots   barotn,
In   the   cave   on   God's   advice

hɔt   main   vaib   dɛm   tɛig   gɜ.ˈknɔ.tn̩
Hot   mayn   vayb   dem   teyg   geknotn."
Has   my   wife   the   dough   kneaded

Tell me, Marrano: Where, and from whom,
Will you get your *matzahs*?
"In the cave, with only heaven to help her,
There my wife has kneaded the dough."

---

zɔg   ma.ˈran   vi   vɛst   zɪx   kli.gn̩
Zog,   maran: Vi   vest   zikh   klign
Tell   Marrano   How   will   you   manage

a   ha.ˈgɔ.dɜ   vu   tsu   kɾi.gn̩
A   hagode   vu   tsu   krign?
A   hagadah   where   to   get

ɪn   dɛɾ   hɛil   ʔin   ti.fɜ   ʃpal.tn̩
"In   der   heyl,   in   tife   shpaltn,
In   the   cave   in   deep   cracks

hɔb   ɪx   zi   ʃɔin   laŋ   ba.ˈhal.tn̩
Hob   ikh   zi   shoyn   lang   bahaltn."
Have   I   it   already   long   hidden

Tell me, Marrano: Where will you manage
To find a *hagadah*?
"In the cave, in a deep crevice,
Is where I've hidden it for a long time."

---

zɔg   ma.ˈran   vi   vɛst   zɪx   vɛ.ɾn̩
Zog,   maran: Vi   vest   zikh   vern,
Tell   Marrano   How   will   yourself   protect

vɛn   mɛn   vɛt   dain   kɔl   dɛɾ.ˈhe.ɾn̩
Ven   men   vet   dayn   kol   derhern?
When   one   will   your   voice   hear

Tell me, Marrano: How will you
Protect yourself
When they hear your voice?

ven der sɔɪ.nɜ vɛt mɪx faŋ.gɜn̩
"Ven der soyne vet mikh fangen,
If the enemy will me capture

vɛl ʔɪx ʃtaɾ.bn̩ mɪt gɜ.'zaŋ.gɜn
Vel ikh shtarbn mit gezangen."
Will I die with songs

"If the enemy captures me,
Then I will die with songs on my lips."

136

17

Zog, maran

Words by Abraham Reisen (1876-1953)
Music by Samuel Bugatch (1898-1984)

Arrangement by Robert De Cormier
(piano reduction by John Yaffé)

Andante pensivo (♩ = 66-72)

p espr.

espr.

ten.

mf

a tempo

Zog, ma-ran, du bru-der may-ner: Vu iz greyt der sey-der day-ner? In

a tempo

ti-fer heyl, in a khey-der, dort hob ikh ge-greyt mayn sey-der, in

a tempo

p

ti-fer heyl, in a khey-der, dort hob ikh ge-greyt mayn sey-der.

B *a tempo*

Zog, ma-ran: Mir vu, bay ve-men, ves-tu vay-se mat-ses* ne-men?

In der heyl, oyf gots ba-ro-tn, hot mayn vayb dem teyg ge-kno-tn,

hot mayn vayb dem teyg ge-kno-tn.

* 'matses': *The unleavened bread used in the Passover seder*

Zog, maran

C
25
a tempo
Zog, ma-ran: Vi vest zikh kli - gn a ha-go - de vu tsu kri - gn?
8va (loco)
a tempo
mf
ped.
29
a tempo
In der heyl, in ti - fe shpal - tn, hob ikh zi shoyn lang ba-hal - tn,
a tempo
p
33
poco rall.
in der heyl, in ti - fe shpal - tn, hob ikh zi shoyn lang ba-hal - tn.
poco rall.
3
ped.
D
37
a tempo
mf
Zog, ma-ran: Vi vest zikh ve - rn, ven men vet dayn kol der - he - rn?
a tempo
mf
p

Ven der soy - ne vet mikh fang - en vel ikh shtar - bn mit ge - zan - gen.

ven der soy - ne vet mikh fan - gen vel ikh shtar - bn mit ge - zan - gen.

Zog, maran

18
Zog nit keyn mol
(or 'Partizaner lid')

This song is perhaps the best known of the Yiddish songs created during the Holocaust. Poet Hirsh Glik wrote the song while interned in the Vilnius (Lithuania) ghetto after hearing the news of the 1943 *Warsaw Ghetto Uprising*.* He based it on a pre-existing melody by composer Dmitri Pokrass, and the song was quickly adopted as the official anthem of the Vilnius *partisans* (the underground resistance movement). It also spread with remarkable rapidity to other ghettos and camps and was translated into several languages. It later spread to Jewish communities all over the world. It is a Brechtian (i.e., Bertold Brecht) march song, unequivocal in its message, and rich in defiant optimism; it acknowledges suffering in the past and present and urges people to continue fighting for their survival. Today, it is sung at almost all Holocaust commemorative gatherings.

Glik was moved out of the Vilnius ghetto and imprisoned in two different concentration camps in Estonia. He escaped and joined the partisans but was killed by the Germans in 1944 in a battle in a nearby forest.

* *Warsaw Ghetto Uprising* (April–May, 1943): The largest, symbolically most important Jewish uprising, and the first urban uprising, in German-occupied Europe. It was an act of Jewish resistance opposing Nazi Germany's final effort to transport the remaining ghetto population to Majdanek and Treblinka concentration camps. Around 13,000 Jews died in the course of the uprising, and the rest of the ghetto inhabitants were deported to the extermination camps.

18
Zog nit keyn mol
(or 'Partizaner lid')

zɔg nɪt kɛɪn mɔl (paɾtizanɜɾ lid)
Zog nit keyn mol (or **Partizaner lid**)
Say not no time (or Partisan song)

Words: Hirsch Glik (1922-1944)
Music: Dmitri Pokrass (1889-1978)

TEXT:

- IPA Transliteration
- **Sung Text**
- Word-for-Word Translation

IDIOMATIC TRANSLATION

---

zɔg nɪt kɛɪn mɔl ʔaz du gɛɪst dɛm lɛt.stn̩ vɛg
Zog nit keyn mol az du geyst dem letstn veg,
Say not no time that you go on the final road

xɔtʃ hɪm.lɜn 'blaɪ.ɜ.nɜ faɾ.'ʃtɛ.ln blɔɪ.ɜ tɛg
Khotsh himlen blayene farshteln bloye teg
Although heavens leadened conceal blue day

vaɪl kʊ.mɜn vɛt nɔx ʊnd.zɜɾ 'ʔɔɪs.gɜ.bɛŋ.ktɜ ʃɔ
Vayl kumen vet nokh undzer oysgebenkte sho,
Because come will still our longed for hour

ɛs vɛt ʔa pɔɪk tɔn ʊnd.zɜɾ trɔt mɪɾ zaɪ.nɜn dɔ
Es vet a poyk ton undzer trot: mir zaynen do!
It will a drum do our step we are here

Never say that this
Is the end of the road for you,
Though leaden clouds
May conceal skies of blue;
Because the hour
That we have longed for is near,
Our steps drum out
"We are here!"

fʊn gɾi.nɜm 'pal.mɜn.land bɪz vaɪ.sn land fʊn ʃnɛɪ
Fun grinem palmenland biz vaysn land fun Shney
From green land of palms to white land of snow

mɪɾ kʊ.mɜn ʔɔn mɪt ʔʊnd.zɜɾ paɪn mɪt ʔʊnd.zɜɾ vɛɪ
Mir kumen on mit undzer payn, mit undzer vey;
We come on with our pain with our suffering

ʊn vu gɜ.'faln̩ sɪz ʔa ʃpɾɪts fʊn ʔʊnd.zɜɾ blʊt
Un vu gefaln s'iz a shprits fun undzer blut,
And where falls it is a spurt of our blood

ʃpɾɔt.sn̩ vɛt dɔɾt ʔʊnd.zɜɾ gvʊɾɜ ʔʊnd.zɜɾ mut
Shprotsn vet dort undzer gvure, undzer mut.
Sprouts will there our strength our courage

From the green land of palm trees
To the land of the white snow,
We're arriving with our pain
And with our sorrow;
And wherever a drop of our blood
Should fall,
There springs forth our strength
And our courage.

dɔs lid gɜ.'ʃɾi.bn̩ ʔɪz mɪt blʊt ʔʊn nɪt mɪt blaɪ
Dos lid geshribn iz mit blut un nit mit blay,
The song written is with blood and not with lead

sɪz nɪt kɛɪn li.dl̩ fʊn ʔa fɔɪ.gl̩ ʔaf dɛɾ fɾaɪ
S'iz nit keyn lidl fun a foygl af der fray
It's not no song from a bird in the free

dɔs hɔt ʔa fɔlk tsvɪ.ʃn̩ 'faln.dɪ.kɜ vɛnt
Dos hot a folk tsvishn falndike vent,
That has a people between collapsing walls

dɔs lid gɜ.'zʊŋ.gɜn mɪt na.'ga.nɜs ʔɪn di hɛnt
Dos lid gezungen mit naganes in di hent!
The song sung with pistols in the hand

This song is written with blood,
And not with lead;
It's not a little song
Sung by a bird overhead.
It is the song of a people
Amidst collapsing walls;
It is sung with pistols
In their hands!

zɔg nɪt kɛɪn mɔl
Zog nit keyn mol...(etc.)
Say not no time

Never say…(etc.)

18
Zog nit keyn mol
(or 'Partizaner lid')

Words by Hirsch Glik (1922-1944)
Music by Dmitri Pokrass (1889-1978)

Arrangement by Robert De Cormier
(piano reduction by John Yaffé)

Moderate march tempo (♩ = 98-104)

1. Zog nit keyn mol az du geyst dem let - stn
(2.) pal - men-land biz vay - sn land fun

veg, khotsh him - len blay - e - ne far-shte - ln blo - ye teg; Vayl ku - men
shney, mir ku - men on mit und - zer payn, mit und - zer vey; Un vu ge-

vet nokh und - zer oys - ge-benk - te sho — es vet a poyk ton und - zer trot: mir zay - nen
fa - ln s'iz a shprits fun und - zer blut, shpro - tsn vet dort und - zer gvu - re, und - zer

Lyrics (measure 8):
do! Vayl ku - men vet nokh und - zer oys - ge - benk - te sho — es vet a
mut. Un vu ge - fa - ln s'iz a shprits fun und - zer blut, shpro - tsn

Lyrics (measure 11):
poyk ton und - zer trot: mir zay - nen do!_____
vet dort und - zer gvu - re, und - zer mut._____

1.
2. Fun gri - nem

Lyrics (measure 14):
2.
B
3. Dos lid ge - shri - bn iz mit blut un nit mit blay, s'iz nit keyn

li - dl fun a foy - gl oyf der fray; Dos hot a folk tsvi - shn fa - ln - di - ke

vent, dos lid ge - zun - gen mit na - ga - nes in di hent! Dos hot a

folk tsvi - shn fa - ln - di - ke vent, dos lid ge - zun - gen mit na - ga - nes in di

poco allarg.

hent!___ 4. Zog nit

poco allarg.

29
C
Slightly held back
keyn mol az du geyst dem let - stn veg, khotsh him-len bla - ye-ne far-shte - ln blo - ye
Slightly held back
(♭)
32
teg; Vayl ku - men vet nokh und - zer oys - ge - benk - te sho — es vet a
35
poyk ton und - zer trot: mir zay - nen do! Vayl ku - men vet nokh und - zer oys - ge - benk - te
3
3
(♭)
38
allarg.
sho — es vet a poyk ton und - zer trot: mir zay - nen do!
allarg.
3
f

'*I swore never to be silent whenever and wherever human beings endure suffering and humiliation. We must always take sides. Neutrality helps the oppressor, never the victim.*'

— **Elie Wiesel**, Nobel Prize-winning author

Robert de Cormier

Robert De Cormier (1922–2017) was an American musical director, arranger, and composer. He graduated from the Juilliard School and subsequently arranged music for many singers and groups, including Harry Belafonte and Peter, Paul and Mary. He and his wife, singer Louise De Cormier, collected and recorded folk songs from the Catskill Mountains of New York, and he also arranged the music for a number of anthologies including *A Book of Ballads, Songs and Snatches* and *The Weavers Songbook*.

De Cormier was the acclaimed music director of the New York Choral Society, renowned for its high standard of excellence in choral singing and unique variety of programming, from 1970 to 1987. As Music Director Emeritus, he then conducted performances of Verdi's *Requiem*, the Berlioz' *Requiem*, and the premiere of Missa Iona, all in New York City. During the 1995-96 season, he conducted two operas composed in the Terezin (Czechoslovakia) concentration camp, *Brundibar* (Hans Krasa) and *The Emperor of Atlantis* (Viktor Ullmann), in performances in Vermont, New Hampshire, Massachusetts, and at Merkin Concert Hall (NYC).

In 1993, he was invited to establish and develop the Vermont Symphony Orchestra Chorus. As its director, he both prepared and conducted Mozart's *Mass in C Minor*, Verdi's *Requiem*, Vaughan Williams' *Dona Nobis Pacem*, Haydn's *Creation*, Beethoven's *Missa Solemnis*, Orff's *Carmina Burana*, and Brahms' *Ein deutsches Requiem*. In 2000, he founded the vocal ensemble Counterpoint, which made its first U.S. tour in 2008. Their CDs include *When The Rabbi Danced, Shalom, Noel We Sing, Missa Criolla, Let Me Fly, Christmas in Vermont*, and *Premieres*.

De Cormier's recordings include three Christmas albums for the Arabesque label (with The De Cormier Singers); the Kodaly *Missa Brevis* and Vaughan Williams's *Mass in G Minor* for Vox Turnabout (NY Choral Society); *Songs of Liberty* for Book-of-the-Month Club (NY Choral Society and De Cormier Singers); *Carmina Burana* for Newport Classics; Paul Alan Levi's *Mark Twain Suite*, De Cormier's *Legacy* and *Four Sonnets to Orpheus* for Centaur, and *Christmastide* with opera singer Jessye Norman for Philips. His most recent recording, *The Prague Sessions* (for Rhino Records) celebrates the life of the late Mary Travers of Peter, Paul and Mary, with orchestrations created by De Cormier for many of their most popular songs, recorded with members of the Prague Philharmonic in the fall of 2009.

A recording of John Dowland's music *Awake, Sweet Love*, with Julianne Baird and the De Cormier Singers, was released by Arabesque, and *Noel We Sing* (NY Choral Society) was a Musical Heritage release. His other Arabesque releases in-clude *Oh, You Beautiful Doll — A Celebration of Tin Pan Alley, Children, Go Where I Send Thee — A Christmas Celebration Around the World*, the operas *Brundibar* and *The Emperor of Atlantis, The Jolly Beggars*, and De Cormier's settings of Robert Burns' poetry.

De Cormier's television credits include a three-part series, *Choral Folk Songs*, for the BBC and an Emmy award-winning special with Harry Belafonte. He conducted *Christmastide* with Jessye Norman for Thames TV, and, for the U.S. Public Broadcasting System (PBS), with Peter, Paul and Mary in *A Holiday Concert, Peter, Paul and Mommy Too*, and *LifeLines*. He was the choral director for a combined concert, PBS television special, and recording starring Jessye Norman and Kathleen Battle. He is also credited as choral director for the PBS Special *Christmas at Carnegie* with Kathleen Battle and Frederica Von Stade.

De Cormier composed music for chorus as well as ballet and Broadway musicals. His ballet score *Rainbow Round My Shoulder* is in the active repertoire of the Alvin Ailey American Dance Theater.

De Cormier served on the New York State Council on the Arts, and was a member of the choral panel for the National Endowment for the Arts. He was presented the Governor's Award for Excellence in the Arts by the Vermont Arts Council, as well as Lifetime Achievement Awards from the NY Choral Society and Choral Arts New England. In 2007, he was awarded an honorary Doctor of Arts degree from Middlebury College and an honorary degree from the University of Vermont in 2012.

About the Author-Editor and Pianist on the Recording

John Yaffé (Ph.D.) is currently Assistant Professor and Co-Course Director for Music at Coventry University (England) and regularly tours the UK and Europe with his wife, Juliana Janes-Yaffé, as part of the *Yiddish Folksong Project*. He hails from New York City, where for more than two decades he was active member of the city's musical community. He conducted at Carnegie Hall, Lincoln Center, Symphony Space, The 92nd Street Y, and most of the city's other concert venues.

Most recently, he was in the Czech Republic, where he led recordings of piano concertos of Frédéric Chopin and Robert DeGaetano. He also led the Stuttgart Chamber Orchestra (on their U.S. tour), the Colorado Springs Symphony, Warsaw Philharmonic, San Antonio Symphony, Chattanooga Symphony, Chattanooga Opera, Walla Walla Symphony, the Turkish State Opera, and, at the invitation of the American Embassy in Tirana, Albania, led the first American musical ever produced in that country (*West Side Story*).

His musical training began with piano lessons at age seven, and continued with composition at sixteen. By age nineteen, he was already composing for educational films and arranging for commercial recordings. He completed his conservatory studies in Los Angeles, where he studied piano with Charles Fierro, orchestral conducting with Lawrence Christianson, and opera conducting with David Scott.

Early in his career, Yaffé was championed by several major figures: the great baritone Tito Gobbi, who invited him as musical assistant for his master classes in Florence, Italy; Julius Rudel, Music Director of New York City Opera, who invited him to join the company as an apprentice conductor; Francis Rizzo, esteemed opera director, dramaturge, and all-around 'opera guru'; the legendary singer George London, who invited Yaffé to join the staff at the Washington (D.C.) National Opera; and Leonard Bernstein, who was Executor of Marc Blitzstein's estate and entrusted Yaffé with revisions to Blitzstein's opera *Regina*. Engagements at the Wolf Trap Festival and with symphony orchestras and opera houses in Maryland, Connecticut, Michigan, California followed.

Soon after, Yaffé moved to Europe. He spent ten years as a répétiteur and conductor in the German opera houses of Hagen, Münster, Osnabrück and Stuttgart. In addition, he served as Music Director of the Stuttgarter Operettentheater and was a guest conductor with the Städtisches Orchester Remscheid, the Südwestdeutsche Philharmonie, the Symphonie-Orchester Graunke of Munich, the Staatsorchester Stuttgart, the Stuttgarter Philharmoniker, the Stuttgart Ballet, and the Alt-Wiener-Strauss-Ensemble. In 1989, he was brought back to the U.S. to lead the burgeoning Florida Philharmonic Orchestra as its Resident Conductor, where he conducted over 175 performances during his tenure.

From 2008 to 2010, he served as Series Producer of the *Sounds of the City* concert series at the New-York Historical Society, Music Director of the orchestra of New York City's prestigious 92nd Street Y (1996-2009) and Encompass New Opera Theatre (1996-2008), as a principal guest conductor at the Mannes College of Music Preparatory Division (1996-2006), and as Co-Director of the Orchestral and Chamber Music Program of the Tanglewood Institute.

He was responsible for the acclaimed restoration of Irving Berlin's *Louisiana Purchase*, performed at Carnegie Hall, and now available on CD. His commercial recording credits include premiere recordings of the orchestral music of Norma Wendelburg, Frank Loch, William Thomas McKinley, Robert DeGaetano and Marvin Schluger. As well, he has produced recordings of the complete piano music of Earle Brown, the complete piano music of Luciano Berio, and the songs of Leo Sowerby.

He has also performed widely in recitals with Juliana Janes-Yaffé, with whom he has recorded German, Italian, and American art song literature for Südwestfunk Baden-Baden.

About the Singer on the Recording

Soprano **Juliana Janes-Yaffé** is a UK-based performer and vocal pedagogue. She is currently a voice tutor and lecturer at Coventry University (England) and voice tutor at Royal Northern College of Music (Manchester, England) Junior Division. Her repertoire has encompassed over thirty opera roles, a broad cross-section of the Italian, French, German and American art song literature, and most of the major oratorio solos. She has worked closely with numerous contemporary composers, inspiring works written especially for her. She has been heard as a soloist in performances at New York's Brooklyn Academy of Music, Lincoln Center Festival, and 92nd Street Y; she has been a guest soloist at the Steirischer Herbst Festival (Austria), Cygnus Chamber Ensemble, the Friends and Enemies of New Music, the Concordia Orchestra, Colorado Springs Symphony, Brooklyn Philharmonic, Dallas Symphony, Oakland Symphony, San Jose Symphony, Florida Philharmonic, Istanbul Philharmonic, Orchester der deutschen Oper Berlin, Tokyo City Philharmonic, Orquestra del Teatro Colón (Buenos Aires), Orchestra dell'Opera di Genova, Orchester der Stadt Münster, Südwestdeutsche Philharmonie, Symphonie Orchester Graunke (Munich), Alt-Wiener-Strauss-Ensemble, Vienna Operetten-Bühne, Orchestra of The 92nd Street Y, New-York Historical Society, and the Walla Walla Symphony. She has sung solo recitals in France, Germany, Italy and Switzerland, as well as throughout the U.S. She is currently active in world-wide performances and lectures in connection with her funded *Yiddish Folksong Project*.

Recently, she has been a featured soloist at the New York City Electroacoustic Music Festival, International Festival of Innovation Music Production (Leeds, UK) Contemporary Music Research Centre (York, UK), Sound+Environment Conference (Hull, UK), Convergence Festival (Leicester, UK), and at the INTIME Symposium (Coventry, UK).

Born in Texas, she received her bachelor's degrees in Vocal Performance and Music Education from Southern Methodist University, and, soon after, was engaged as a soloist at the Municipal Theater in Münster, Germany. In the twelve years following, she was a full-time contracted Principal Soloist also in the opera houses of Essen and Stuttgart. Guest engagements found her in San Francisco, New York, Darmstadt, Aachen, Osnabrück, Kassel, Berlin, and Miami. In 1992, she resumed her postgraduate studies, receiving her Master of Music Degree in Vocal Performance and Pedagogy from Boston University, where, as a Dean's Scholar, she was a protégé of the renowned Phyllis Curtin. During that period, she also served as a vocal instructor, both in the Boston University School of Fine Arts, as well as its Tanglewood Institute.

Ms. Janes-Yaffé has recorded (with her husband, conductor/pianist John Yaffé) songs of Stefano Donaudy, Lee Hoiby and Arnold Schönberg for Südwestfunk (Germany). Alongside her performing activities, she was (from 1995 to 2014) Head of Vocal Studies at the Mannes College of Music Preparatory Division, New York City, and she was for nine years on the voice teaching staff at New York University, where she also headed the courses in German and French Lyric Diction for Singers.

About the Violinist on the Recording

Violinist **Adam Summerhayes** was brought up steeped in varied folk idioms, became a concerto soloist and a specialist in early music, and he effortlessly moves between those disciplines — whether it is twentieth-century chamber music or his playing of unaccompanied works by Bach.

He received turtoring from both the great pedagogue Yfrah Neaman and his grandfather, a violinist and fiddler who learnt from Adolf Brodsky (who premiered Tchaikovsky's **Violin Concerto**) and a direct link to the greats of a golden era of violin playing and a long line of North Country fiddlers.

Adam started his international career playing solo concertos in prestigious venues such as the Hermitage Theatre in St Petersburg and the Rudolfinum in Prague. Much of his career has been devoted to chamber music, kick-started by a Southbank Centre Purcell Room recital of music by Aaron Copland and Alan Bush, culminating in critically acclaimed premier recordings of music by those composers. He has since recorded twenty-five discs for various labels including Harmonia Mundi, Meridian Records, Chandos, ASV, Toccata Classics, Sargasso, and Red Priest Recordings. He now has his own label, Extinct Records.

He has also performed many times in the Queen Elizabeth Hall and Wigmore Hall and recently played in distinguished international venues including the Beijing Central Conservatory of Music Concert Hall, Théatre du Chatelet, Paris, and the Metropolitan Museum in New York. His extensive international touring has taken him to France, Spain, Portugal, Switzerland, Austria, Germany, the Czech Republic, Scotland, Northern Ireland, Poland, Croatia, Saudi Arabia, Finland, Denmark, Russia, China, Canada, Luxembourg, Holland, Belgium, Alaska, and the U.S.A. Fiddle playing has also taken him from folky improvisation on small stages at Glastonbury to the 02 Arena in London (with the Dutch pop sensation Caro Emerald).

Adam's fiddle playing defined his role in Zum, the touring gypsy-tango band that created what became a new musical genre, and for which he wrote much of the music. His new project, Dodo Street Band, combines elements of the traditional tunes he played with his grandfather to create a wildly irreverent exciting take on folk music, encompassing melodies from the shores of the Hebrides to the mountains of Eastern Europe. He performs with Cormac Byrne, the word renowned bodhrán player, and their recording 'Stone Soup' was released in 2019.

In 2015, he joined the avant-garde Baroque quartet Red Priest, with which he spends a large portion of his time touring. (He arranged and composed most of the group's latest disk *The Baroque Bohemians*, which topped the classical music charts.)

His arrangements and compositions feature on twelve other discs, perhaps most notably Harmonia Mundi's *Piazzolla and Beyond* and Chandos's *Gypsy Strings*. This led to a composition for the soundtrack of Guy Ritchie's 'Sherlock Holmes: A Game of Shadows', in which Adam makes a cameo appearance as a gypsy. He also improvised and recorded a melancholy melody as actor Robert Downey Jr.'s body double before training the actor to mime to the resulting track. He also plays medieval gemshorns, mandolin, mandola, and a Hammond 44 melodion, instruments that feature in his Dodo Street Band and his duo Ciderhouse Rebellion.